Georgia Rivers

GEORGIA
RIVERS

Articles from the Atlanta Journal and Constitution Magazine

Edited by

GEORGE HATCHER

UNIVERSITY OF GEORGIA PRESS - ATHENS

CONTENTS

ILLUSTRATIONS

The illustrations are by staff members of the *Atlanta Journal and Constitution Magazine*. Photographs for all rivers except one by Kenneth Rogers, Chief Photographer. Photographs for the Coosa River by Floyd Jillson, staff photographer. Maps by Bob Connell, art director.

FOREWORD

HAPPILY, contained here between these covers are the stories of the rivers of Georgia.

Rivers, of course, are the stuff of dreams. A boy stands on the bank of one and watches its movement. Somewhere, he knows, its waters will reach the sea. His imagination is stirred with a dream of ships and travel, of strange, foreign lands, and adventure. An old man, standing beside the flow of a river, sees in it a symbol of eternity—the waters rolling forever toward some unseen end of a journey.

The engineers look at a river and see dams to generate electricity, lakes to provide reservoirs and recreation for the great and growing cities, water for irrigation, a coolant for the machines and processes of huge and mysterious factories and plants. Transport managers see long strings of barges moving heavy goods and grain, connecting the interior of America with the oceans and the markets of all the world.

So it is with the rivers of Georgia. If we have had no river decisive in history as were the Ohio and the Mississippi, our rivers have not lacked historical influence and significance. Indeed, until the publication of this volume, Georgia has paid scant attention to her rivers. Relatively little has been written about them. Yet, they have all played a significant role in the story of our state. There are novels yet to be written about the days when the Altamaha and the Savannah were black with long rafts in the time when the vast hardwood forests of the Southeast were cut with a ruthlessness painful to read about. The Chattahoochee was an almost silent river of history. It was her fate to be a convenient border in early boundary disputes and in the last years of the far-spread Creek Indian Nation. For years after the tribes were conquered in other regions east of the Mississippi, the Creeks were settled in Georgia and what is now Alabama and a part of Mississippi. A treaty made by General Oglethorpe in the Indian villages of the Chattahoochee made possible his victory at Bloody Marsh, a victory that put the stamp of Britain rather than Spain on the land.

The romance of the rice plantations along the St. Marys River and the stories of the time when the sailing vessels from Europe were crowded at her docks also await the novelist.

Now, in the last decades of the twentieth century, we see that Georgia's rivers are to play an even more prominent role in the industrial civilization. We are just in the edges of it, and already we know that rivers are essential for transport, for industry, for the uses of cities, and for the planned, industrialized agriculture which will be needed to feed the populations of the future.

We are indebted, therefore, to Mr. George Hatcher, editor of the *Atlanta Journal and Constitution Magazine*, for his decision to publish a series on the rivers of Georgia, and to the University of Georgia Press for bringing the stories together in this volume.

Ralph McGill

SAVANNAH

By William Hammack

In her wild old days, the Savannah River ran red with mud and blood—blood of Indians and Spaniards, Frenchmen and Englishmen, Americans, heroes and cowards, sinners and saints. She's still pretty muddy, but the cough of guns on her waters has been replaced by the snicker-chuck of diesel tugs busy with commerce. From the ordeal of battle, she has come to a striving for peace—on her north bank, some of her children are making material which serves as a deterrent to war, although it can wreak devastation more terrible than her early sons could have dreamed of. The Savannah and her tributaries drain more than 10,000 square miles, an area that receives some of the heaviest rainfall in North America.

There is something about a big river that lures a man and there is something about the Savannah that holds a man close to her. Talk to Captain Frank W. Spencer, who started out

William Hammack was born in southwest Georgia and was graduated from the University of Georgia with an A.B. degree. He went to work as a waterfront reporter for the *Savannah Morning News*, and after serving in World War II, studied at New York University. He was a reporter on the *Moultrie Observer* before joining the staff of the *Atlanta Journal and Constitution Magazine* in March 1953. He is married and has a daughter and a son.

on the river in 1899 and knows her as few do, who was Master Pilot of the port of Savannah for 30 years, and you'll see love for her in his eyes and hear it in his voice as he speaks of her.

This river of many moods, this changeable river—she's a businesswoman transporting millions of dollars' worth of cargo, she's a gay companion to water sports lovers and fishermen, she's a playgirl, singing a siren song at night, dressed in black velvet spangled with diamond glitter from ships' lights—was known by early Indians as "Isondega" or "Isundiga," which means "blue water."

For a Savannahphile, it is hard to believe that the river ever was clear. A prominent Georgia historian who loves her, Alexander A. Lawrence of the city of Savannah, has written: "No doubt it was much clearer before the white man turned the forested, red clay hills into fields and plantations but intensive research has failed to discover that any early traveler in Georgia ever described the Savannah as being blue or clear."

Georgia was born on the river—rivers are the spawning beds of civilization; our first records come to us from the Tigris, the Euphrates, the Nile. The first white man to see the Savannah was Hernando de Soto, who with his band of 600 men reached her in 1540. De Soto pressed on in his thirsty quest for the gold of El Dorado. He found not El Dorado but death, and was buried in another river, the Mississippi.

In the late 16th century, the French started the first European commerce on the Savannah, trading with the Indians for sassafras. Sassafras tea, as a medicinal drink, swept Europe as a fashionable fad. Sassafras may be said to have caused the first naval battle on the river. In 1603, Spaniards, who were irate at what they deemed French transgression in Spanish new world territory, fought French traders on the river; the French, outmanned, were defeated.

The Spaniards called the Savannah the "Rio Dulce"—sweet river. The Westoes called her "Westobou"—river of the Westoes. The Westoes were Indians who lived along her banks and were allies of the English, acting as a buffer tribe against the Spanish to the south, protecting the colony at Charleston in Carolina. Around 1682, a branch of the Shawnees, the Savannahs, savagely fell upon the Westoes and drove them from the river, succeeding the conquered tribe as British allies.

The English traded with the Indians, bartering guns and cloth for furs and deerskins. Trade flourished. Vast herds of deer minced in the woods; they were slaughtered for their hides, which were shipped by pack trains and flatboats down the river and around the inland waterway to Charleston, thence to England. The deerskin trade grew until just before the American Revolution, when it stopped—the deer had been nearly wiped out.

The very zeal of the white traders as they went about their business, ruthlessly exploiting the Indians, resulted in a violent uprising, the Yamassee War of 1715, that almost forced white men from the river. This near toppling of British rule led to the establishment of a rampart to buttress the Carolina colony on the south—the settlement of Georgia.

General James Edward Oglethorpe was an aristocrat who became enraged when a friend, a brilliant man who couldn't handle money, was thrown into prison for debt and died there of smallpox. Oglethorpe headed an inquiry into the jail system, and the dreadful conditions found and reported by his committee resulted in the release of thousands of debtors. However, they were little better off, because they couldn't make a living in overcrowded England. Oglethorpe suggested a way to help them, while at the same time serving the ends of empire—send the debtors to America to form a new colony south of Charleston. His idea met with resounding approval—it was humanitarian, appealing to religious leaders; it was tactically sagacious, providing as it would a strong buffer against the Spanish, and thus pleasing to government chiefs; and it was plain good business.

Never did a colonial venture attract more attention. Hundreds applied but only a few could be chosen, and Oglethorpe screened applicants with great care. Finally, 35 families were selected. Although it was contemplated originally to set up the new colony for debtors, by the time the charter was granted, the scope of the plans had widened to include other unfortunates. Dr. E. Merton Coulter, the distinguished historian, has written: "Probably not a dozen people who had been in jail for debt ever went to Georgia."

Oglethorpe and his colonists reached Charleston on January 13, 1733, and after he picked a site for the new city of Savannah, on a 40-foot-high bluff 18 miles upriver, the 35 families landed at their new home on February 12. With the help of a great and wise chief of the Yamacraws, Tomochichi, the settlement prospered. Another who assisted Oglethorpe was a half-breed woman, Mary Musgrove. Later, she turned on the colonists, calling herself Mary, Queen of the Creeks, and only the alertness of Captain Noble Jones at the head of his small army saved the city from Mary's warriors.

In 1735, Oglethorpe established Augusta, which he named for the mother of George III. His choice of the far upriver location was influenced by the profitable trade with the Indians that went on in a trading post opposite the site of Augusta, Savannah Town, which had been set up early in the 18th century by English fur traders from Carolina.

Georgia grew; in 1772, acting Governor James Habersham wrote: "It is with Inexpressible Satisfaction that I see this Colony making so rapid a progress to Wealth and Importance."

When the American Revolution blazed up, the British quickly saw the strategic importance of the city of Savannah. Anthony Stokes, His Majesty's Chief Justice of the Province, described the city as "the key of the southern provinces and the Gibraltar of the Gulf passages." In December 1778, 3,000

Redcoats landed, commanded by Lieutenant Colonel Archibald Campbell, Lieutenant Colonel John Maitland, and Sir James Baird of the 71st Regiment of Scots Foot. On the 29th, the city fell. Colonel Campbell and his victorious army swept up the river, meeting small but fierce resistance from handfuls of patriots commanded by John Twiggs and William and Benjamin Few. But these lion-hearted men were hopelessly outnumbered, and in January, Colonel Campbell took Augusta.

In an attempt to free the valley from the British, American General Benjamin Lincoln with his army and French Count d'Estaing with his great fleet launched a two-pronged attack on the city of Savannah, from the land and from the sea. But the allies lost, with heavy casualties. One who was killed was Count Casimir Pulaski, the valiant Polish general.

The tide started to turn in 1782, when General Light-Horse Harry Lee captured Augusta. General Nathanael Greene, commander of the Southern Department, and General "Mad Anthony" Wayne surged on to conquer the British; in July, 1782, General Wayne's army stepped high through Savannah streets.

The children of the river had been knocked down by the war—farms were laid waste, money was worthless, homes were ruined. They were down but not out. They did not weep over what they had lost. They went to work. Soon rice and tobacco were flourishing and the flatboats were running the river.

Then Catherine Greene, widow of the general, invited Eli Whitney to her home along the river, Mulberry Grove, which had been given to General Greene by a grateful Georgia. When Whitney invented the cotton gin, he crowned King Cotton and he lit a fuse that ignited the Civil War. King Cotton needed many hands and he kept slaves in bondage, creating one of the issues that turned brother against brother for four grievous and bloody years.

In the days following the War of 1812, Augusta became

the cotton center, sending cotton downriver on big cotton rafts to Savannah, a white flood that lined with gold the pockets of plantation owners, merchants, and shippers. In the harbor, sailing ships waited to take the bales to England. In 1818, the value of Savannah's exports was more than $14,000,000. Savannah River businessmen were enterprising and forward-thinking; they helped sound the knell of all the vessels that rode the seas with the wind—the stately full-rigged ship, the lean and lovely clipper, the graceful schooner.

In November, 1808, the citizens of Augusta goggled at a ship that chuffed upstream with smoke billowing from her smokestack—the first steamboat on the river, the brain child of William Longstreet, an Augusta inventor. The year he died, 1814, Samuel Howard was given by the legislature exclusive rights to run steamboats on the Savannah and all Georgia waters, and he put a steamer on the river in 1819, the year the first transatlantic crossing was made by a steamship.

In May, 1819, the steamer *Savannah*, financed by 21 city of Savannah businessmen, stood from the harbor and paddle-wheeled downriver to reach the ocean, cross it, and, wearing a proud plume of smoke spangled with sparks like fireflies, dock at Liverpool in June.

In the following years, the muddy waters of the river were churned by steamboats that grew progressively more luxurious to satisfy the increasingly sybaritic tastes of the children of the river who were getting richer and richer on cotton and trade. Canny boat owners also saw to it that there was plenty of space for lucrative cargo. Sometimes there were 15 paddle-wheelers a week running between Savannah and Augusta.

The river can be gentle and the river can be mean—she trapped boats on sandbars she suddenly built up, and like a petulant jade, she moved her channel. By 1865, 11 of her boats had sunk, six had blown up, and 13 had burned.

In the '60s, the river knew other vessels—fighting ships.

Before the fingers of the Federal blockade strangled the Savannah port, the steamer *Fingal* slipped into the harbor, bringing the richest contraband cargo of the Civil War—14,000 Enfield rifles, 1,000,000 ball cartridges, 2,000,000 percussion caps, 1,000 short rifles, 500 revolvers, and 400 barrels of cannon powder. When Fort Pulaski fell, the harbor was stoppered and the *Fingal* was bottled up. She was converted into an ironclad, and rechristened *CSS Atlanta*. This unwieldy man-of-war steamed to Wassaw Sound in June, 1863, and engaged two Union monitors. The ironclad was killed.

In his book about the Savannah, Thomas L. Stokes wrote: "The Savannah River valley was, in truth, the Mediterranean of the Confederacy, providing it with men and ideas." Among the greats were Alexander H. Stephens, vice-president of the Confederate States of America; Robert Toombs, Confederate secretary of state and later a general in gray; and Howell Cobb, a Confederate general.

Though Fort Pulaski fell in April, 1862, the river mouth's defenses protected her nearly to the end. Fort McAllister, for example, withstood nine attacks by the Federal Navy, and was not taken until December, 1864, when General William Tecumseh Sherman arrived at the sea at the end of his march through Georgia. A few days after McAllister's capture, Sherman occupied Savannah. The Federal Navy had strangled the South with its blockade. Now Sherman had gutted the Confederacy.

Several months later, Jefferson Davis, president of the conquered CSA, was captured in Irwinton, Georgia, and Alexander Stephens was arrested at his home in Crawfordville. They were taken to Augusta, where they were put aboard a tugboat. The vessel steamed downriver to Savannah, and Davis and Stephens were escorted to the steamship *Clyde*, to be taken north to prison.

The river valley had not been put to the torch by Sherman as had Georgia country in his line of march, but the children of the river drank the same vinegar of defeat and ruin as their inland brothers had to drink. Slowly the valley came back to life. Cotton was selling for a dollar a pound at the end of the war, but now the price started to drop, reaching four cents a pound by the '90s. Still, this was cotton country, and the bales kept on going down the river. Soon, however, two new products appeared on the muddy waters—naval stores and lumber. In 1883, the president of the Board of Trade wrote that "12 years ago a barrel of rosin or spirits of turpentine was scarcely known in this market, while today Savannah is known as the largest naval stores market in the world." Captain Frank Spencer recalled that in 1900 "The square riggers came in for naval stores, the schooners loaded lumber, while the tramp ships picked up cotton cargoes."

Trees grew tall and thick in the swamps below Augusta, and in the closing years of the 1800s the need for timber created a big lumbering industry. Raftloads of logs floated downriver for years; after a time, rafting was the only activity on the river—the railroad had taken the place of the steamboat.

And industry took the place of cotton. Marked changes on the lower river started in 1915 when representatives of the sugar industry came to Savannah to find a site for a sugar refinery. It was built several miles upriver, after Captain Spencer assured company officials that ocean-going vessels could be navigated that far.

Captain Spencer, a licensed Master and Marine Engineer of United States ocean-going vessels, opened the channel in the Upper Harbor in 1917. The opening was an epochal event. It stretched the harbor an additional four miles, making room for present-day plants. Among the industries on the river are paper and paperboard, petroleum, sugar, chemicals, and gypsum.

The riverfront is busy and bustling and booming, with Captain Spencer's diesel tugboats towing and butting deep-water ships into and out of the harbor. His big towboat *Savannah* dwarfs her oldest sister the *Cynthia*, an 80-year-old veteran of the waterfront, but the *Cynthia* is still as sprightly as ever. During the Spanish-American War she was chartered by the Associated Press to serve as a dispatch boat. She has become a tradition on the river.

Of all the traditions of the riverfront, the most widely known among mariners of the seven seas was the "Waving Girl." In 1887, Florence Martus started waving at every vessel that passed Elba Island, where her brother was lighthouse keeper. She waved a handkerchief in the daytime, a lantern at night. The "Waving Girl" left Elba in 1931, and no longer did her friendly handkerchief flutter or her welcoming lantern gleam.

Savannah handles more general cargo than any other South Atlantic port, as W. H. McGowan, executive secretary of the Savannah District Authority, pointed out. Up and down the riverfront, there are four active terminals—two operated by the Georgia Ports Authority and two by private firms—four general cargo berths and many oil and private berths. Through November, 1960, the port handled 1,143.3 million pounds of exports valued at $112.5 million, and 3,479.3 million pounds of imports worth $91 million.

Upstream is the giant Savannah River plant of the Atomic Energy Commission, where materials for man's most destructive weapons are made, and where studies are conducted on nuclear benefits for peaceful purposes. The water pumped daily from the river for use in the plant's nuclear reactors would supply a city of several hundred thousand persons— Savannah, Augusta, and Hartwell also drink from the river.

But "all work and no play" is not true of the river—never has been. Never before have so many enjoyed pleasures the stream offers. In 1946, the United States Army Corps of Engineers went to work on the great Clark Hill Dam, more than a mile long and 200 feet high. The dam, 22 miles upstream from Augusta, reduces flood damage, increases the depth of the navigation channel from Augusta to Savannah, and generates hydro-electric power. The mighty inland sea that is Clark Hill Reservoir—with a shoreline of 1,200 miles—provides fun-filled opportunities for fishing, boating, water-skiing, and swimming. Disciples of Izaak Walton who flock to the lake catch bass, bluegill, crappie, shad, yellow perch, and other fish.

Fishermen cast and water sports lovers frolic on another vast body of water on the upper river, the reservoir created by the Hartwell Dam, seven miles below the confluence of the Tugaloo and Seneca rivers, which join on the Georgia-South Carolina line a few miles northeast of Hartwell to form the 314-mile-long Savannah. From that point, on its winding course to the Atlantic, the river marks the boundary between Georgia and South Carolina. With a 960-mile shoreline, the Hartwell Reservoir spreads over 61,900 acres. Hartwell's power generators were designed to produce an average of 453 million kilowatt hours annually.

Another Corps of Engineers project provides a channel nine feet deep and 90 feet wide from Augusta to Savannah, with Clark Hill and Hartwell reservoirs assuring minimum flow requirements. The principal commodities that ride the river today are petroleum products upstream and brick downbound. The barges, passing places with such names as Poor Robin Landing, meet pleasure craft on the river; and new sailors, who generally are exceedingly salty in speech, are loud with "Ahoys!" The Savannah has heard many tongues since the days when she listened only to the Indians—the lilt of Spanish and French, and soft, slurred Geechee talk—and she has known many children, her own and those who became adopted as soon as they met her.

She has been changed. She has been tamed; no more will she breach the levee at Augusta to batter the city as she did in the 1929 flood. She has been deepened; when General

Oglethorpe navigated his craft up the river to the site of Savannah, the depth of water between sea and site was a scant nine feet at low water—today a low water depth of 34 feet prevails, with a tide rise of seven feet. The Corps of Engineers has been improving Savannah Harbor for more than a century, and while the engineers have been working on the river a long time, they plan many more developments. Clark Hill Dam and Reservoir was the first to be constructed under an approved general plan of eleven dams for development of the Savannah River basin.

But with all the changes, the Savannah is still herself, a big river that works hard and plays hard as she lazes down to the sea.

.. 2 ..

~~~~~~

OGEECHEE

~~~~~~

By Andrew Sparks

IF the Mississippi is Old Man River, Georgia's Ogeechee is a lady—mother, sweetheart, harlot, a beauty, and a plaything. The lady hardly earns a livelihood. Some Georgia streams work for their keep—generating electricity, carrying freight, backing up behind dams that fatten the rivers into great multipurpose lakes. But the wild, unspoiled Ogeechee does almost nothing, like some pampered darling—which it is for fishermen.

The 250-mile-long river extends from Greene County southeastward to Ossabaw Sound, where it flows into the Atlantic Ocean between the islands Ossabaw and Wassaw. For much of its course the river is extravagantly beautiful. Touring the Ogeechee is an adventure in sight-seeing, and can be done two ways, by boat and by car.

By boat, paddling quiet as Indians or scooting along scaring terrapins with an outboard, you fathom the river's soul, meet its family of snakes, alligators, high-jumping silver mullet,

ANDREW SPARKS was born in Birmingham, Alabama, but his family moved to Georgia when he was four and he grew up in the river town of Millen, on the Ogeechee. He received A.B. and M.A. degrees from the University of Georgia and taught English at North Georgia College in Dahlonega before he entered the service in World War II. In 1945 he joined the staff of the *Atlanta Journal and Constitution Magazine*. He is married and has a daughter and a son.

13

and quick darting redbreasts. You glory in the beauty of its shining black water, and absorb the lady's perfumes—magnolias, bream beds, honeysuckle, and the rich smell of black muck drying in the sun. You glide through a moving, sun-splashed cathedral of arched oaks, gums, and bays. Willows hang green curtains at the windows and tall, fat-bellied cypresses edge out into the water. On the Ogeechee, riding the current, you flee from civilization into an almost uninhabited world, deserted except for an occasional fisherman.

Clark Hill Reservoir at sunset.

Clark Hill Dam on the Savannah, 22 miles upstream from Augusta.

Hartwell Dam, seven miles east of Hartwell.

One of the headstreams of the Savannah, the Tallulah River, shown north of Lake Burton in northeast Georgia.

Diesel tugboats on the busy waterfront at Savannah.

Georgia's Ogeechee River has no better friend than Mrs. Shed Dickerson of Chatham County.

The Walter Meeks home on the Ogeechee near the coast.

The Henry Ford home, built in the 1930s, facing the Ogeechee River.

The Ogeechee leaping the rocks at Shoals.

King's Ferry Landing on the Ogeechee below Savannah.

The Altamaha near its mouth.

Tom and Hughes Howard fishing in one of the many shaded sloughs along the Altamaha.

Dame's Ferry on the Ocmulgee between Forsyth and Gray.

By car, you see a very different river as you wind your
way up from the coast to the old ferry sites, cross rattle-trap
wooden bridges scarily labeled "Load Limit, 3,000 Pounds,"
and scoot over wide, smooth concrete spans of the big tourist
arteries that cross the river—U.S. highways 17, 301, and 1.
Along all the roads you find the people who inhabit the river
lands. You meet the folks, past and present, who loved the
Ogeechee best.

Henry Ford was such a man. He bought nearly 80,000
acres of Ogeechee land in Bryan and Chatham counties near
the coast, built a mansion house, and tried to change the
economy of the section. The reason? Mrs. Ford hated south
Florida and wanted a winter home where she could raise
grass. The Fords have gone now, but the grass in front of
their mansion house is lush and green, spread out like wall-
to-wall carpeting from the white columns of the house to the
black water of the river. The lawn has 300 or 400 hidden
drains from which surplus water is pumped to a sump pit
concealed in a reconstructed rice mill and from there is pumped
into the river.

"It's pure crab grass, some centipede, and some St. Augustine," said Marvin L. Sharpe, who has been caretaker of the
property for 32 years and for four different bosses. "Ford
told me, 'Sharpe, let's get something green here. Mrs. Ford
wants a green pasture.' Before long he had 25 trucks hauling
in the sod.

"I don't expect Mr. Ford knew what a fish hook was or
ever shot a gun. He stayed busy when he came here. He had
close to 1,000 men working on the place, a big saw mill running and a lot of land in cultivation. He tried to get everybody
a home around here. He had an engineering room in the re-
built rice mill and always brought two engineers with him.
The first Ferguson Ford tractor ever built was put together
right here. And when they changed from A Models to V-8s,
the plans were discussed here for two or three years before
the change was made.

"Sherman destroyed the original house on the site, but the Fords tried to put their house, built of bricks from the old Hermitage in Savannah, as near as possible on the spot where the old one stood. They moved into it in 1936, and filled it with very expensive furniture, all of which has been sent back to Michigan. Between visits, Mrs. Ford used to lock up $150,000 worth of crystal and chinaware in the butler's pantry. The doors have a system of electric locks so you can push a button to open the door if you get locked inside.

"One chandelier, Mr. Ford told me, cost $65,000. Only one man was allowed to touch it. His name was Devores and he was the master mechanic of the entire Ford Motor Company. When the chandelier needed dusting, he came down from Dearborn to do the job. And when the house was closed after Mrs. Ford died, Devores came down to pack it up. Mrs. Ford was hardboiled as granite rock."

Ten years ago, the International Paper Company bought Ford's Ogeechee River farm for close to $5,000,000, including the mansion house and some 160 other buildings, most of which have since been sold. Gilbert Verney, an industrialist from New Hampshire who married R. J. Reynolds' sister, bought the mansion and leased some of the river land to a group of Texans who grew Georgia's last crop of rice around 1953. The house was then bought by Mrs. James W. McCook of Macon, who raises purebred Aberdeen Angus cattle on pastures in the reclaimed rice fields. The paper company, on its land which includes 15,000 acres of marsh, grows pines for pulpwood.

In 1958 the paper company gave the State of Georgia a 32-acre tract not far from the mouth of the river, the site of Fort McAllister, where the Confederates almost cut off Sherman's supply ships. Years ago, Mrs. Ford restored the old ovens in which food was cooked at the fort. The State Historical Commission now hopes to restore the whole fort and to build a museum and a caretaker's house, if it gets the necessary $75,000 which was approved by the last legislature.

Along the river, between the fort and the Ford house, are still a few old columned houses. One of the last downstream on the river and one of the few remaining ante-bellum Ogeechee River plantation houses near the coast is Folly Farms, home of Mr. and Mrs. Walter W. Meeks. Coming on the house unexpectedly at the end of a sandy road in the swamp is like finding a Shangri-La, Old-South style. If a visiting Yankee, including Sherman, ever wanted the perfect picture of the romantic South, this is it, with moss, magnolias, white columns, head-high banks of azaleas under the oaks, and a brick-walled garden overgrown with old-fashioned shrubs and ivy. The big 110-year-old house has 14 bedrooms, but Mr. Meeks has an Atlanta apartment, commutes to an office there, and travels all over the Southeast.

As you go up the river, crisscrossing it on the highways, it seems that time piles up like driftwood about the old fords and landings. The Ogeechee, like any other river, is an attic, a catch-all of history, an anthology of fishermen's tales, a Boccaccio collection of characters who have lived upon it, fought and fished it, died, and risked their lives in its coffee-colored waters.

You could expect to find historic ghosts at King's Ferry Bridge, where Georgia's coastal highway crosses the Great Ogeechee, as the stream was called in colonial days. There American Colonel John White—the "hero of the Great Ogeechee"—became a kind of Sergeant York of the Revolution when he captured 111 British troops, and five vessels and their crews of 40 men. Unlike sharp-shooting York, White didn't fire a single shot when he captured the Tories.

Those Tories, trying to reach Savannah, which was held by the British in the late summer of 1779, took refuge in the Ogeechee, disembarked, and fortified a camp on the river bank. Colonel White devised a brilliant plan to capture them with a total force of seven men. He had his soldiers build watchfires all through the woods to make the Redcoats think they were surrounded. That night the seven weary Americans marched from fire to fire, challenged themselves as sentinels, whispered imaginary orders to imaginary troops, and rode off on horseback like busy staff officers. The British thought they were trapped by a large force of Americans by the time Colonel White dashed into camp, alone, and demanded that they surrender. His bluff worked, and the British captain had already surrendered when a second American galloped up on horseback, by prearranged plan, and demanded to know where to place the artillery.

"Keep them back," Colonel White answered. "Move your men off and send me three guides to conduct the British to the American post at Sunbury."

Years later, William Tecumseh Sherman, hot and bothered after the long walk from Atlanta, became frustrated at this same river crossing. The Ogeechee was almost his undoing. The Yankee general's army of 60,000 men had fared well in the rich farmlands of central and eastern Georgia, eating off the fat of the land as they burned the houses and looted the farms, but in Chatham County they found only rice and rice straw. For the siege of Savannah Sherman needed heavy guns and all classes of supplies for his men and animals. Those supplies were just beyond his reach, anchored in the mouth of the Ogeechee on ships which could not get past Fort McAllister, which the rebels had thrown up in 1861 and 1862 to guard Savannah's "back door." All attempts to reduce the fort by naval bombardment had failed.

Sherman ordered General William Hazen's division to cross the Ogeechee at King's Ferry Bridge and attack from the rear, via Bryan's Neck Road. The red-haired Yankee general stood on the opposite bank of the river at a rice mill and watched the fort fall. Then he opened communications with the Federal ships anchored in the sound and got on with his job of capturing Savannah for Mr. Lincoln's Christmas present.

King's Ferry Bridge is quiet now, except for the groan of

trailer trucks and whiz of tourists' cars speeding to or from a Florida vacation. The acrid odor of a paper mill mixes with the sea breeze and with the brown smell of hushpuppies frying at Love's Fishing Camp. Across the road, the shiny cars and boat trailers of fishermen fill the parking lot at King's Ferry Park, built and maintained by the International Paper Company. A sign erected there almost sounds like a slogan for the river: "This park is dedicated to your pleasure and happiness. May restful and carefree hours of relaxation spent here renew your zest for worthwhile living."

All up and down the river the wet spring and summer of 1961, people complained that the water was too high to fish. Mrs. Shed Dickerson, who runs Uncle Shed's fishing camp in Chatham County upstream from King's Landing, says, "I've put on 20 pounds, the fishing's been so bad. I ain't had anything to do but set and watch the water go by." Mrs. Dickerson and the Ogeechee she loves so well both had roles in a Hollywood movie, "Cape Fear," filmed in Georgia. She had a bit part, but the river was a star, languishing a tantalizing kind of beauty in front of the Hollywood cameras and showing off 30 miles of charm all the way from King's Ferry to Morgan's Bridge near Ellabell.

At Mrs. Dickerson's the river is black and swift when the water's high, sequined in the sunlight, fanned by gray moss, walled in by green and chartreuse trees. From across the river fishermen can hear the thunder of Fort Stewart's guns.

"The fort stretches from Morgan's Bridge to Canoochee down at King's Ferry—that's 32 miles and it's a heap of the river. Army folks let you sit in your boat and fish on their side, but they won't let you land. Two boatloads of MPs were in here this morning, tacking up signs on the other bank. I own five miles of the river myself and two lakes, Big Elmer and Little Elmer. Hit's a pretty river—the prettiest one there is. I said when I came out here I'd live and die here, and when I leave the river, I'm going out feet first."

No main highway parallels the Ogeechee any more, like the old River Road that was one of Georgia's earliest routes west of the river and led from Savannah to Georgia's frontier. It followed an old Indian trail up to the present site of Bartow and turned west, later connecting Savannah and the state capital Milledgeville. You can find bits and pieces of the old road still, but the sand is deep in places, the stagecoach inns are closed or gone, and filling stations are almost non-existent.

Anywhere you stop there's a story. Emory Lane, who lives in Blitch, grew up in a tollgate house. His daddy once owned the 10 bridges that cross the river and the swamp between Blitch and the town of Ogeechee. "I've seen the time when it took a man steady opening and closing the gate to let the traffic through," said Mr. Lane. "The toll for a horse and buggy was 20 cents, for two mules and a wagon was 35, and for a man on horseback was a dime. Fishermen got through free. Later there were free bridges at Rocky Ford and Dover and our business naturally went down. My father gave Bulloch and Screven counties $1,000 apiece to take over the bridges and make this a free crossing in 1916. We kept a better bridge than we've got now."

Oysters, they say, did in a man named V. H. Burns who lived in Ogeechee, Georgia. They weren't Ogeechee River oysters, but ones that arrived by passenger train in the high water year of 1925. Raging flood waters of the river stopped Savannah trains at Ogeechee, and Mr. Burns ate some dining car oysters that had been off the ice too long. He "took ptomaine and died that very day." Mr. Burns had run the town's only hotel in a day when traveling salesmen came by train and rented a horse and buggy to make their rounds of country stores.

The spookiest place you can find on the river is John Randolph Cooper's house, hidden in a tangle of vines high on a hill above the river, at Ogeechee. The town lost its postmaster, station master, and express agent the day Mr. Cooper died. He had all three jobs. At his house, deserted now, the blinds are shut, but peeks through them reveal a darkly mysterious interior with shadowy outlines of furniture, lending credence to the rumor that the house is haunted.

Douglas Parker, who runs Ogeechee's only store, says the ghosts were invented by college students from Statesboro and other young people who have invaded the house for parties.

On the Ogeechee side of the river, the Central of Georgia Railroad follows the crooks and turns of the river all the way up past Wadley. State Route 17 parallels the railroad from a point between Eden and Bloomingdale, up through Guyton, Egypt, Halcyondale, Ogeechee, Rocky Ford, Scarboro, Millen, Herndon, Midville, and Louisville, Georgia's third capital which was laid out near the river in 1786, with its plan copied from that of Philadelphia. Other paved roads follow the Ogeechee up through Grange, Edgehill, Shoals, Jewell, Mayfield, and Powellton to Union Point, where it rises. The Ogeechee's a "county" river. It doesn't come close to a town with more than 3,500 people and most of the towns are far from that. It is also Georgia's biggest river with the same name from its source to the sea.

It may be Georgia's laziest.

Back in the 18th century the Ogeechee spun and carded wool and cotton and cut wood as industriously as an energetic farmwife. Shoals on the Ogeechee, a town now almost deserted and forgotten, had a waterpowered woolen mill and iron foundry in the 1790s when an industrialist named Bird came down from Virginia, put up factories, and built his family a house called "Aviary." The Bird house is gone now and all that is left of the mills at Shoals is stone pillars sticking up here and there in a grove of poison ivy. Sherman burned the mills.

Miss Minnie Coleman, a blonde music teacher in Warrenton,

is the daughter of the man who owned the mill. "My father was from Virginia," she said, "and he must have been 13 or 15 when he came to Georgia. 'I was so poor,' he said, 'I had to wear Cousin Harper's socks.' But before he was 30 he had bought every bit of the property at Shoals, 2,000 acres of land and Cousin Harper's house above the river. The dam broke in my teens. A new one would have cost $25,000 and father just kept patching and fooling with it. People used to clamor for meal from the Shoals. You know, the bigger the rock, the finer the meal. He peddled it all over the country from Macon to Augusta."

The Ogeechee's only miller at the river's only mill is Binion Griffin, who runs a mill at Mayfield, owned by the Reynolds estate. He hauls the Ogeechee River meal, he says, to Warrenton, Crawfordville, Camak, Norwood, Barnett, Culverton, Sparta, "and all the grab-alls between here and there."

At Shoals, a few miles down from his mill, the languid old lady Ogeechee becomes a chattering mountain girl, blushing for the first time with the red of Georgia clay. The old gal gurgles among big boulders, churns over rocky slopes, splits at an island, and foams white in eddies and whirlpools under the willows. Down at the water, the endless rush of the river wears away the rocks as imperceptibly as time. Relics of all the people who have passed are there, souvenirs of the old gal's lovers: an unfinished flint arrow some Indian threw away when he was tempted to swim instead of work; the granite millrace of Bird & Hamp, which was cut in the solid rock by burning pine logs on it and then dashing cold water on the hot stone.

The Ogeechee has lovers all the way to its source in Greene County, near Union Point. The actual source of the river is debatable.

"Everybody with a spring claims that's it," says J. B. Dolvin of Greensboro, who owns one of the springs himself on his father's old home place between Union Point and Siloam. "There's a spring right at the head of my pasture that a lot of folks say is where the river starts. But three different springs come together just below my place and there's another one that flows through Union Point."

In 1960, Mr. Dolvin built a dam above his barn and a 2½-acre pond, now stocked with bream and bass. Soon, he says, all it will need is a good fisherman.

Georgia's Ogeechee, the fisherman's darling, couldn't be born in a better place than a fishpond.

.. 3 ..

ALTAMAHA

By Willard Neal

The raging Altamaha is Georgia's mightiest river in the volume of water it carries to the sea. Its bed is about the widest, its deep holes are the deepest, and its swampy shores are the wildest. It harbors sturgeons weighing 350 pounds or more and carrying up to 80 pounds of excellent caviar. Shrimp boatmen testify that its delta creeks are jumping with tarpon from June through August.

Tributaries of the Altamaha sweep down through the middle of Georgia, robbing fields and gardens of their richest topsoil and depositing it as black muck in the famous marshes of Glynn and McIntosh counties. One finger drained the old frog pond in which the magic stake was driven to mark the center of Terminus, that grew into Atlanta. This branch flows into South River, which joins Yellow and Alcovy rivers in Jackson Lake, where they give the power generators a spin and run out under the dam as the Ocmulgee. The big river flows on by Macon, Hawkinsville, Abbeville, Jackson-

Willard Neal was born at Holly Pond, Alabama, and was graduated from the University of Alabama with an A.B. degree. He worked on newspapers in Decatur and Birmingham, Alabama, and in St. Petersburg and Clearwater, Florida, before coming to the *Atlanta Journal and Constitution Magazine* in 1926. He is married and has one son. The Neals live on a farm in Fayette County.

ville, and Lumber City, and joins the Oconee to become the mighty Altamaha.

The Oconee rises near Lula, just over a ridge from the Chattahoochee River, and flows down through Athens, picks up the Apalachee, joins Little River in Lake Sinclair and generates some electric power, then skirts Milledgeville, runs through Dublin, and collides head on with the Ocmulgee.

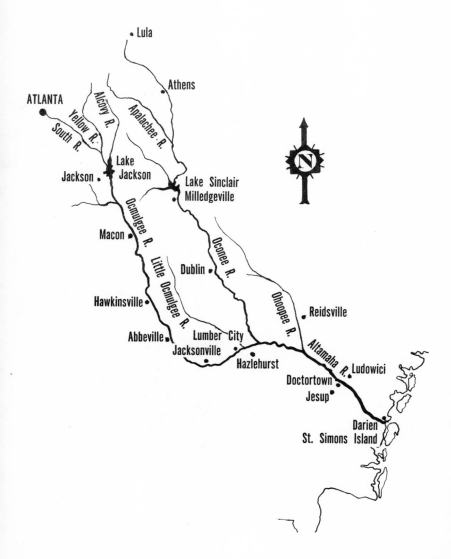

The Altamaha's water is wild and shiftless. Whereas the Chattahoochee, Savannah, and Coosa have been harnessed to turn many generators and mill wheels, the only licks of work done by the Altamaha system are at Jackson and Sinclair, and a number of grist mills on the upper creeks. However, its teeming delta annually produces several million dollars worth of seafood.

For a hundred years, during the steamboat era, the old river was a main highway for hauling freight between Macon and Savannah. J. C. Hadden, who operates a cotton gin, peanut mill, and fertilizer business at Hawkinsville, believes he is the last of the licensed pilots. "Except for Mark Twain, few rivermen ever did much writing, so history of steamboating on the Altamaha in the old days is pretty skimpy," said Captain Hadden. "However, the river valley changed very little, so I imagine it was always about like I knew it.

"The last line in operation was the Macon-Atlantic Navigation Company, which owned the steamboat *Greater Macon*, and the diesel *Ocmulgee*, that I ran. The round trip took two weeks, so we had a boat at each terminal port once a week, and the middle river had the services of two boats a week.

"We ran work barges, not fancy packets. My only passengers were occasional fellows who went along for the adventure. We could carry 200 or 300 tons, and we were nearly always loaded. There usually was more business than we could handle. In Savannah we took on groceries, hardware, sugar, and fertilizer; and put off cargo at Darien, at Doctortown, which was the port for Jesup and Ludowici, and at Lumber City, Jacksonville, Hawkinsville, and Macon on the Ocmulgee, and at Mount Vernon and Dublin on the Oconee. Then we loaded cotton, naval stores, and lumber for the return trip. We carried a lot of local freight from the railroads to big farms along the river. It wasn't unusual to tie up to the bank and set out 200 bags of fertilizer. In the prohibition era we'd sometimes set off a couple of hundred pounds of sugar.

"We didn't haul liquor. However, we'd sometimes see fires burning up the creeks at night, or pass through blankets of smoke coming out of the swamps. Before outboard motors, the folks along the river mounted Model-T engines in oversize bateaux. They broke down pretty often and we'd give them a tow. They always said they were fishing, but there was rarely any tackle in sight.

"The only fish we knew about were catfish and carp. There must have been bass, bream, and crappie in the water, but people had not learned how to catch them."

The scheduled boats shared the river with a few steamboats engaged in hauling logs to big sawmills, and countless rafts of enormous logs being floated down to Darien.

"The rafts had no power and little steerage way, so we would pull out of the channel and let them go by," said the captain. "In high water they would sometimes get caught in a suck, which is what they called being pulled into the trees when the current took a short cut through the woods. The only way to get loose was to be towed out by a steamboat. Sometimes they'd be stuck a day or two before we came along. We never charged for pulling them out.

"The railroads never hurt us. In fact, we worked together. But when the highways were paved, motor trucks put us out of business, in 1934.

"The Lindquist Lumber Company at Lumber City bought the boat, *Ocmulgee*, and I went to work for them. I had my only wreck there, with the *Dorothy T*, carrying a full load of logs. I was coming down the Oconee and through a rock channel just above Bell's Ferry when we hit a submerged log that was jammed in the rocks. It ripped out a good section of our bottom. We settled on firm sand, with the entire barge under water, but the cabin standing up dry. I left the crew in the cabin, paddled the skiff to shore, and hitched a ride in a log truck the six miles to Lumber City. Then I ran the *Ocmulgee* around the forks and up the Oconee, and took all the

logs and machinery out of the sunken boat, and towed the
hull out to a sandbar, where its skeleton can still be seen in
low water."

Rafting logs down to Darien was a lifetime calling for some
of the old rivermen. The late "Turkey" Thompson of Hawkinsville said in olden days they would cook fatback, potatoes,
and corn pone on the rafts going down, and walk back with
their guns, living on game. Later, rafters made the return trip
by rail.

Byron A. Thompson of Lumber City, a retired mail carrier,
rode a raft down 50-odd years ago. "I guess this country pro-
duced cypresses and longleaf yellow pines as big as ever grew,"
said Mr. Thompson. "Green cypress is too heavy to float.
Loggers would ring the trees to kill them and let them stand
to dry out a year before cutting them down. Before tractors,
the log cart was used—a wide axle with wheels nine feet high.
One end of a log was hung from the axle, and four or more
oxen dragged the timber to water.

"The raft I rode was two lengths of 75-foot pine logs
about 30 feet wide. I don't remember how many logs there
were, but they were nailed in place with boards. We had a
tent in the center, a box of sand for the cooking fire, and a big
rudder at front and back. The crew consisted of three men.
We went down without stopping, in three days and two nights,
and passed several rafts tied up to trees at night. It's a crooked
river. The crewmen said that sometimes on clear nights they
could hear other rafters talking 40 miles downstream—but
only two or three miles away or less through the woods.

"Sometimes the current would throw two or more rafts
together and break them up, and then things got hectic. The
men would have to sort out their own logs and nail up the
rafts again, while the old river tried its best to scatter the
pieces or swing the whole mess into another collision.

"The men I was with sold their logs at Darien. A big saw-
mill there used all it needed, but most of them were towed to

Savannah or Brunswick. I expect Altamaha timber built most of those two towns, and probably a lot of houses in New York and England."

B. K. Halstead of Hawkinsville recalls seeing a lot of shipmasts being prepared near his town about 1926. "They were yellow pines 90 feet long without a knot, and they had to square 14 inches at the butt," he said. "The loggers squared them with adzes, then rode them to Darien where they were turned at a ship fitters' plant.

"Rhodes Landing, a big slough just above Hawkinsville, was a natural collecting place, where logs could be corralled while rafts were being made up," Mr. Halstead continued. "It's also the home of whopping striped bass. I've weighed several from there that went over 35 pounds. Three or four years ago the owner of the property died of a heart attack on the bank, and when they found him a 27-pound fish was still on his line.

"Speaking of big fish, about 10 years ago a Negro drowned below town, and when they discovered him there was a line tied to his big toe and a 47-pound catfish on the hook."

As soon as the new colony at Savannah was well established, General James Edward Oglethorpe brought over 150 Scottish Highlanders to build Fort King George in the Altamaha delta, and the nearby town of New Inverness, now Darien, in 1735. The next year Fort Frederica was started on St. Simons Island. Visitors today are amazed at the tremendous amount of dirt the old soldiers moved in digging moats and erecting embattlements. Furthermore, Oglethorpe had his King George garrison dig a canal three-quarters of a mile long across Brett's Island, which cut 16 miles off the rowing distance between Darien and Frederica. The work paid off in 1742 when the Darien soldiers hurried down to reinforce Frederica and there defeated Spanish invaders in the Battle of Bloody Marsh, one of the decisive engagements in our history, since it ended Spain's dream of conquest to the north. Gen-

eral's Cut, as the canal is called, is used today as a short route
by shrimp boats. The marshy land beyond is called General's
Island.

When not building forts, digging a canal, and fighting
Spaniards, the Darien soldiers amused themselves shooting
golf on what was probably the first course in America.

The big farms around Darien set the style for plantation
life in the Old South. William Bartram, the famous naturalist,
was entertained at the McIntosh plantation in the 1760s.

Bartram did a stupendous job of listing and describing the
plant life of Georgia. For one of his trips he borrowed a canoe
at Darien and took a 50-mile solo paddle up the Altamaha.
He was enamored of the wild magnolias in the area. One
of the specimens that he took back to Philadelphia, a variety
of bay tree, he named the gordonia Franklinia. Descendants
have become a popular garden tree, but none of the variety has
been recognized in the swamp since. The popular name now
is "lost gordonia," and people are still looking for it.

The naturalist wrote that earlier settlers found the high
ground cleared for 30 or 40 miles up and down the coast,
and 15 or 20 miles up the river, where Indians had farmed. He
said the Creeks claimed their people had come from the west
across the Mississippi and had been fought by local tribes all
the way through the South until they reached the Atlantic,
where they had to stop and make a stand. However, instead
of fighting, they joined their neighbors, and eventually organized all the Southeastern tribes into the greatest confederacy of any primitive peoples. Another interesting Bartram note was that the noisy guns of the white men had already
affrighted all the buffaloes and elk out of Georgia, except that a few elk were still reported to be in the Cherokee
mountains.

The Creeks thought their exodus took place at about the
time the Carolinas were settled, around 1670. However,
modern archaeologists believe it was nearer the period of
De Soto's tour of the state, a century and a half earlier.

The Altamaha delta from high bridge on **U. S. Highway 17.**

Shrimp boats at Darien on the Altamaha delta.

The 150-year-old Archibald Clark house in St. Marys. The oak commemorates Washington's inauguration.

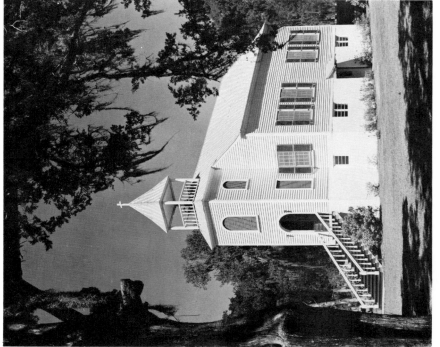

St. Mary, Pембrтокe, Church Lake Moss and the Mangrove

The Suwannee just outside the Okefenokee Swamp.

Amicalola Falls in Dawson County, the highest falls in Georgia. The Amicalola River is a tributary of the Etowah River.

The Coosa River is formed by the juncture of the Oostanaula, left, and the Etowa at Rome.

The oldest Indian relics include exquisite Folsom spear points chipped by the wandering hunters who roamed Georgia for 5,000 years prior to the Year 1. The Ocmulgee National Monument across the river from Macon is a restored Indian town of 1,000 years ago, and one of its principal features is a very fine fall-out shelter built a thousand years before it was needed. This is a council chamber with seats for 50 representatives, entirely covered with several feet of packed clay. The thick walls and roof probably were intended to foil eavesdroppers, but they would also serve well as a shield against radiation. Archaeologist John Walker said the great ceremonial mound is almost identical with the famous Aztec mounds of Mexico, except that the Aztecs veneered their great pyramids with a layer of stone.

The Creeks had their troubles. In 1715 they tried to drive settlers out of the Carolinas, but could not get their armies properly organized and lost the Yamassee War. Pursuing Carolinians burned the mound villages and the Creeks withdrew to the Chattahoochee.

The great swamps of the Altamaha, Ocmulgee, and Oconee have changed very little since Indian times, except that the virgin cypresses and pines have practically all been floated down the river, and the buffaloes and elk were frightened away. The rest of the animals are still there. Recently a wild bear wandered out on the clipped greens of the Ocmulgee Monument. Panthers and wildcats leave their tracks on sand ridges. Rattlesnakes up to seven feet in length are reported, and numerous moccasins writhe among the cypress roots.

Thirty years ago the wild turkey, America's most delicious native bird, was practically extinct except in a few remote areas, but they remained plentiful in the Altamaha Swamp and on Georgia's Golden Isles, and many were trapped in those strongholds to restock forests all over the nation. Tom Howard, who owns extensive swamps and woodlands along the north bank near Ludowici, took us down for a view of the real

Altamaha country. As we rounded a bend in the well-scraped
sand road, a wild turkey crossed in front of us. We saw plenty
of turkey tracks, snake tracks, and gopher tracks, and were
informed that alligators probably saw us, although we saw
none of them.

We paddled bateaux through cypress and tupelo trees into
a slough which extends several miles out from the river. It is
important to look back every few yards and remember what
you see, in order to find the river again.

"People still get lost," said Mr. Howard. "A fellow spent
the night in the swamp near here recently, and he was a
gibbering case of nerves when he was found. I won't say I have
never been lost, for there have been times, on my own land,
when I didn't know which way my home or the river lay.
If clouds obscure the sun and there is no wind blowing you'd
better have a compass. The low sand ridges run in every di-
rection. If you go downhill you run into a swamp. If you try
to follow a ridge it will run out and you're going downhill
again. It can be pretty confusing, and it grows worse if a
fellow gets panicky."

Travelers see the mighty Altamaha at only five places,
from bridges that have high arches over the channel to per-
mit the passage of big boats. It flows about 80 air miles from
just below Lumber City to Darien, but the water distance
around its many crooks and turns is two or three times as far.
For the most part, the south shore cuts steeply against high
sandy-clay country, so the bank may rise abruptly 20 to 50
feet. The north shore merges with the swamps, and has low
sandy banks or knobby-kneed cypresses growing right out of
the water. Its mouth is a 20-mile-long delta, where the water
flows around and among myriads of islands. The river's many
outlets have been called the finest fishing waters in the world.

Phil Cannon, of the State Game and Fish Commission, is
director of the new waterfowl reserve covering 19,000 acres
of the delta islands and marshes. In spring and summer

his crews plant the old rice paddies in grain crops for clouds of migrating ducks and geese to harvest in winter. "The marshes are the richest soil anywhere," said Mr. Cannon. "Down here it brings $3 an acre. If we could move it to Atlanta it would be worth $2,000 an acre for growing produce and flowers."

He scooped up a handful of black mud. It was as fine and smooth as thin flour paste. "Hardly a grain of sand in it," he said. "Sand drops in the channels and washes out to sea. This is the very richest top soil and clay of middle Georgia, stolen by the river and filtered out in the marsh. School children shape it and set it in the kitchen stove and cook it into usable dishes, the way the Indians made theirs. It would be the finest of ceramic materials if a way was found to bleach out the dark, dirty color." The muck is almost bottomless. Several years ago a big caterpillar tractor bogged down, and sank out of sight while workers were trying to rescue it.

The marsh grass, which looks knee high when seen from a distance, turns out to be head high when you get amongst it. Mr. Cannon thinks it would make succulent and nutritious cow feed if anyone could figure a way to cut and cure it. Wild rice grows up through it as tall as upland corn, with leaves almost as broad.

Butler Island, headquarters for the waterfowl reserve, was made into a rice plantation by Pierce Butler, a general on Washington's staff, shortly after the Revolution. The place prospered to the extent that the general could retire to Philadelphia. About 1838 his grandson, Pierce Butler II, came down to rebuild the place, and had 1,100 slaves working there. Then the bottom fell out of the rice market, blamed on the preference of Europeans for home-grown Irish potatoes, and the plantation went bankrupt.

Pierce II's wife, English actress Fannie Kemble, kept a diary which was published during the Civil War as anti-slavery propaganda, and created a sensation. And his overseer, Roswell

King, founded Roswell, Georgia, a flourishing town 20 miles above Atlanta.

Colonel Tillinghast Houston, who made his fortune with a Cuban sugar plantation and later owned the New York Yankees, bought the island in the '20s and tried growing lettuce and asparagus, without much success.

An addition to the old plantation is Egg Island, the last bit of land on the coast opposite the delta. At high tide it is about 50 yards wide and 400 yards long, and was presented to the state by the Sea Island Company. In summer the island is a giant incubator for sea birds. Gulls, terns, sandpipers, black skimmers, and other ocean fowl flock there by the thousands to lay and hatch their eggs in the white sand. Pelicans are usually present, too, but they are very secretive regarding their domestic life. There is said to be a $100 reward for the first person to find a pelican nest.

Darien, on the delta, has long boasted of its shrimp harvest —3,864,000 pounds in 1960, according to figures of the U.S. Bureau of Fisheries—and 200,000 pounds of shad were netted up the Altamaha that year. In late spring the boatmen net sturgeons, giant primitive-type fish weighing up to 350 pounds and producing up to 80 pounds of fine caviar. In midsummer the Atlantic tarpon come rolling through the delta. Darien people claim they have the finest tarpon fishing on the entire coast, and the best waters are within a mile of the Highway 17 bridges.

In 1954 the coast was alarmed by the sudden death of thousands of fish in the lower Altamaha. The exact cause never was determined. A new chemical plant up the river, to be on the safe side, installed a huge settling basin to predigest waste material before releasing it into the stream. No large-scale tragedies have befallen the fish since.

When the rains come, and stay and stay, the Altamaha must handle all the water that falls on the middle section of Georgia, and the river spreads beyond all bounds. With only two small dams away up country to stay the flow, the main stream must take the floods as they come. After a long wet spell in 1958 investigators of the U.S. Geological Survey, Surface Water Branch, reported that the Altamaha was flowing through all the bridges for seven miles along U.S. Highway 25, which means, essentially, she was seven miles wide, with the higher ground in the valley standing up as islands.

The mouth of the big river churns continuously; it is never still. Normal high tides at Darien run eight or nine feet, and when an east wind is pushing the sea water up against the river's volume, the rise may be another foot or two. Currents in the delta are so rapid that boatmen find it important to time their trips with the ebb and flow. The mighty Altamaha even bosses men.

. . 4 . .

ST. MARYS

BY KARL FLEMING

DARK, deep, and lazy flows the St. Marys River to the sea through extreme southeast Georgia. It is a quiet and peaceful stream whose stillness is broken only by the sound of wild birds and the wind whispering in moss-strung trees. Save at the port town of St. Marys on the ocean, there is no commerce upon it. Most of it traverses vast and lonely pine forests, off the beaten paths, and its shores are visited only by occasional fishermen. But the quiet St. Marys has played an important role in the history of Georgia, and many controversies, armed and verbal, have raged around it since its discovery by the white man some 400 years ago.

France, England, and Spain jousted for its control many years ago. It was once a principal trade artery, with many busy landings and docks. It was a favorite hangout for pirates when Spain owned Florida. And in more recent years, Florida and Georgia have carried on a running verbal battle over where it originates.

KARL FLEMING, a native of North Carolina, was graduated from Appalachian State Teachers College at Boone. He worked on newspapers at Wilson and Durham, and came to the *Atlanta Journal and Constitution Magazine* from the *Asheville Citizen* in March 1958. In Asheville he served as state editor and assistant city editor. In 1961 he joined the *Newsweek* regional staff in Atlanta. He is married and has three sons.

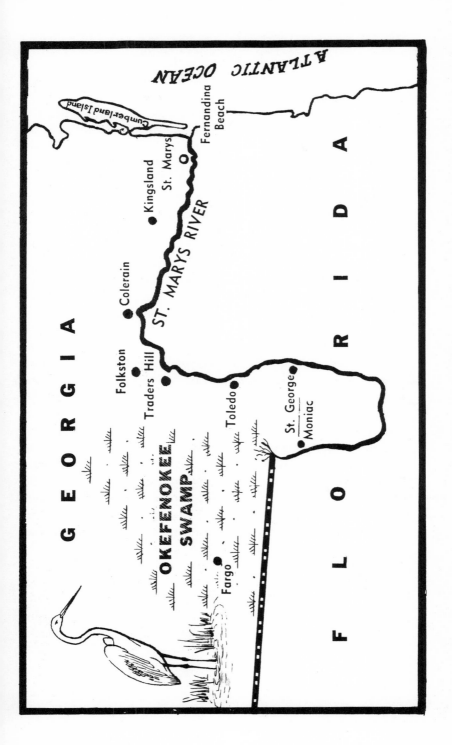

Florida says the St. Marys is formed by several small streams in the northeast section of the Sunshine State. Georgia claims that the St. Marys, like the Suwannee, springs from the waters of Billy's Lake and Big Water Lake deep in the heart of the vast Okefenokee Swamp. Some, on the other hand, say the St. Marys is formed by waters from both Georgia and Florida. From the Okefenokee, whose waters unquestionably do form at least part of the river, the St. Marys flows 180 crooked miles to the sea, between Cumberland Island and Fernandina Beach. Its path forms many miles of the border between Georgia and Florida.

Some historians believe that the first white man to see the St. Marys was Hernando de Soto. His expedition reached what is now south Georgia in 1542. In his journal, De Soto mentioned finding a river and swamp, which many researchers believe to be the St. Marys and Okefenokee.

But if De Soto did find the river, he did not establish a settlement upon it. Neither did a French explorer named Jean Ribault, who landed at St. Augustine early in 1562 and sailed north along the coast until he reached the mouth of the stream on May 1. In honor of the date of this landfall, he called the stream "The River of May." Spaniards later twisted this name into St. Marys.

Ribault and his crew of French Huguenots ventured some distance up the river, and were immensely struck by its unusual beauty. Ribault wrote: "After we tarried, we entered [the river] and veued the country thereaboute, which is the fairest, frutefullest and pleasantest in all the worlde, habonding in honney, veneson, wildfoule, forrests, woodes of all sortes, palme trees, ceders, bayes, the hiest, greatest and fairest vynes in all the worlde, with grapes accordingly, which naturally and withoute man's helpe and tryming grow to the tops of okes and other trees that be of wonderful greatness and height, and the sight of the faire meadowes is a pleasure not able to be expressed with tonge, full of herons, corleau [ibises], bitters [bitterns], mallards, egerles [egrets], woodkockes and of all other kindes of small birds, with hartes, hyndes, buckes, wild swyne and sondery other wilde beastes."

Two years after Ribault's visit, another Frenchman, one Rene Laudonniere, explored the river and established a settlement on it, near the present town of St. Marys, called "La Caroline." But in less than a year the settlement was wiped out when Pedro Menandez, a Spanish admiral, attacked with a sizable armada. The Spaniards held forth until Oglethorpe settled Georgia in 1732-33 and the English Crown claimed possession of the southern coastal area. In the ensuing 30 years, the Spanish gradually lost power, and ceded their rights to England in 1763.

Meanwhile, the Timucua Indians who were on the river when the white man came, were lost in the shuffle and driven out.

By the late 1700s and early 1800s the St. Marys had become an important navigational artery. During this period, hundreds of boats were built on the St. Marys. Sailing schooners and, later, steamboats plied up and down the river, hauling lumber, turpentine, cotton, hides and furs, rice, and dried beef to the sea, and bringing in necessities for the settlers— cloth, powder and shot, sugar, salt, flour, and coffee. In the period between 1810-1820, St. Marys was the fifth largest town in Georgia, and was a principal port on the Atlantic seaboard.

St. Marys was the first sizable town on the river. It was formed on land held before the Revolution by wealthy English gentlemen. But these coastal lands were confiscated by Georgia after America's successful bid for independence, and were awarded to patriots. The town site of St. Marys, reported in various sources at 1,620 to 1,682 acres, was purchased by a group of proprietors from Jacob Weed of Cumberland Island in 1788. They paid him $38 for it. The port and town grew rapidly. Rich rice and cotton planters from the sea islands shipped their goods from St. Marys. Plants for processing forest products sprang up. There were times, during the Spanish possession of Florida, when more than 200 square-rigged vessels could be seen in the harbor and river at once.

Up the river, more landings built up. Traders Hill, near Folkston in Charlton County, was an important Indian trading post until after the Revolution when marauding Indians from Florida subjected it to such numerous attacks that it weakened and gradually died away. Today, all that is left is an old cemetery and a highway marker. Colerain, in extreme southwest Camden County, was the site of a government store put up in 1796 to trade with the Creek Indians. Center Village, south of Folkston, was an important trading post for settlers from Ware, Pierce, Appling, and Coffee counties, who brought furs, beeswax, hides, cotton, dried beef, pitch, and dried peas to Pinckney's Landing and exchanged them for staples. Center Village was on the old "King's Road" and it flourished until the coming of the railroad between Savannah and Jacksonville badly hurt the river traffic.

St. Marys is the only one of the river towns to survive. It was overrun by the British in the War of 1812, being a young town little prepared to defend itself. But its citizens banded together into packs of guerrillas and harassed the British constantly. The town survived at least two epidemics of dread yellow fever, brought in by visiting ships, and was set afire in 1862 by the 9th Maine Regiment in the Civil War. Unable to defend themselves against enemy gunboats, most of its citizens already had fled upriver to Traders Hill. Many did not return after the war.

In the late 1800s, thousands of loads of lumber were sent down the river. Much of it went to Bath, Maine, for the ship building industry. The river was navigable for 59 miles from its mouth but rafts carrying logs and turpentine could be floated down from 70 miles. The St. Marys is known as one of the deepest rivers for its width in the United States.

Not only trading vessels took advantage of the river in the old days. Pirates did too. One of the most famous of the stories about St. Marys, and it is supposedly true, concerned a smuggling vessel that entered the river one day during the time when Spain held Florida. St. Marys had a customs house, and a band of very watchful agents—so watchful, in fact, that the smuggling vessel, loaded with gin and rum, was unable to unload. That night, however, the story goes, some of the smugglers sneaked to the home of the Presbyterian minister, the Reverend Horace Pratt, and removed his horse from its stall. They carried the horse to the church and hoisted it up into the church belfry. Next morning, the whole town was attracted to the scene, and while everybody was occupied in trying to extricate the horse, the smugglers unloaded their goods and sped to sea on the ebb tide.

Today St. Marys is still much the same town, in appearance, as it was long ago. Many of its historic old buildings have been preserved under coats of gleaming white paint. Its sea trade now consists of a little shrimping activity. But the town, owing to the arrival some years ago of a paper and bag company which employs about 3,000 persons, is growing again.

But otherwise the St. Marys River gives promise of being no more than a beautiful lazy stream undisturbed by progress, flowing darkly to the sea with many secrets of past glories buried beneath its surface—the same stream it was 400 years ago when the Frenchman Ribault wrote of its "cunys, hares and gunyea cockes in marveles numbre."

. . 5 . .

SUWANNEE

By Karl Fleming

Way down upon de Swanee ribber
Far, far away,
Dere's wha' my heart is turning ebber;
Dere's wha' de old folks stay.
All up and down de whole creation,
Sadly I roam,
Still longing for de old plantation,
And for de old folks at home.

THOSE words and the sadly haunting melody that accompanies them made the Suwannee River, which rises out of Georgia's wild Okefenokee Swamp, one of the world's most famous rivers.

Yet, ironically, Stephen Collins Foster, the tragic songsmith who died penniless and unhappy in 1864, never saw the river made famous in his song "Old Folks at Home."

At the time he wrote it, in 1851, Foster was composing songs for Christy's Minstrels. He had the melody and most of the words for the song written, but couldn't think of a harmonious river name for the opening line. He wanted one in the South, that had two syllables in it. His brother, Harrison, suggested "Yazoo." Foster said "Yazoo" wouldn't do; it already had been used. So Harrison dragged out a map of the United States and they began fingering the names of Southern rivers. When Harrison pinpointed the Suwannee, his brother

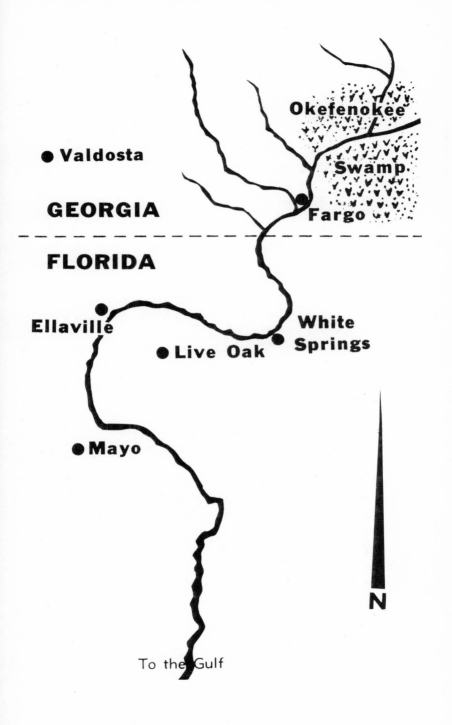

stopped him. That was it. So it was by mere chance that
Foster wrote of the Suwannee and made it probably the most
cherished, nostalgic river in America.

But though he never saw it, Foster managed to paint a
poetically perceptive picture of the Suwannee—lonely, sad,
haunting, darkly beautiful—a place to make the heart tremble
with uncertain longings and wistful dreams.

The Suwannee bubbles out of swamp springs, dark like
strong tea, and winds 200 slow miles to the Gulf of Mexico,
southwest of Gainesville. It leaves Georgia about 10 miles
southwest of the little town of Fargo on the edge of the
331,000-acre Okefenokee Swamp. Cypress, pine, oak, gum,
and tupelo trees, full of moss and mistletoe and squirrel nests,
thickly line the Suwannee shores. Many cypress trees grow
in the water itself so that in some places the river is split up
into many small channels, barely navigable in a small boat.
More than 200 species of birds live along the river, including
cranes and herons. At least two big alligators reside in the
river near its headwaters at Billy's Lake. One of them is 15
feet long, and he can be observed quite often, sunning himself
on a mud flat. The river abounds with fish—bass, bream,
blue gill, perch, catfish, mudfish—and is a favorite of anglers.
C. W. Smith, a serene pipe smoker who lives beside the river
below Fargo, happily recalls catching a 10½-pound bass in
the Suwannee on a flyrod.

Mr. Smith's is one of the few families that actually live on
the river in Georgia. He resides with a sister, Mrs. Sarah
Touchton, whose family homesteaded a 650-acre tract of
land along the Suwannee 100 years ago. They live in a huge
wood-shingled old house with a wide front porch and a cone-
shaped roof, a stone's throw from the dark Suwannee. They
still operate an old horse-powered cane mill for syrup, and
raise hogs that run free in nearby pine woods.

Mr. Smith, who has done a little of this and that to sus-
tain himself for 60 years, now divides his time between farm

chores and hunting and fishing along the water. He thinks
the Suwannee is the most beautiful river in the world. He has
seen it at high water and low, and has been all the way to its
headwaters by boat from the Touchton landing—a distance of
40 miles.

About the oldest family living on the river is that of the
brothers Griffis, Lem and Buddy, who operate a small fishing camp west of Fargo. In 1856 their forebears homesteaded
the land on which the present fish camp lies. Buddy Griffis,
who is 71, tells of how his grandfather, J. G. Mixson, entered
the swamp with his bride over 100 years ago and lived under a
shelter until he could build a log house, held together by
wooden pegs. "I never saw him with any store-bought clothes,
except shoes," Buddy Griffis recalls. "They lived off the land,
grew a few little crops, but mostly fished and hunted. There
used to be plenty of deer and wild turkey in the swamp, but
they're mostly gone now. Granddaddy didn't have a gun, but
he got plenty of game, anyhow. They caught turkeys in
pens. To get deer, he would find a place where they jumped
the fence, and would drive sharp-pointed stakes into the
ground on one side of the fence. When a deer jumped, he
would be stuck on the sticks. We've lived back in here all of
our lives, and there isn't any finer place in the world to be.
In the spring when everything blooms, there isn't any spot as
beautiful as the river."

Along the water, and in it, golden heart lilies, blue hya-
cinths, drooping yellow bonnets, and lavender blossoms of
water shield grow in colorfully rich profusion.

The brothers Griffis champion the virtues of the river
and swamp. And they are champions in another area as well
—tall tale telling. Lem Griffis, who is 65, points to an old muz-
zle-loading rifle on the wall of a little swamp museum he and
Buddy have, and describes how old it is and how long he's
had it. "I got that gun 'way back yonder when it was just
a pistol, and it's grown up into a rifle."

Buddy tops that whopper with one about swamp mosquitoes growing to such vast size and power that screen wire offers no protection whatever against them. "Those fellows tear the tails off lightning bugs and use them as torches to burn through the screen. They drink Flit for breakfast and if you don't watch them close they will grab the hounds and fly off with them."

Except for electricity and macadam roads, the river area around the Okefenokee has been pretty much untouched by progress. The houses are weather-beaten, unpainted pine board affairs, some hanging precariously on the river bank. The river people live simply and unhurriedly and a psychiatrist would starve to death among them.

Scouting the river, we drove along a sandy road and drew up to a landing fronted by an open wooden gate. A sign on the gatepost announced: "Blow horn for service." Fifty feet from the gate there sat a little unpainted clapboard cabin. On its front porch, a man clad in overalls sprawled asleep in the sun, a tattered hat pulled down over his eyes. When we blew, he raised his head slightly, tilted his hat, paused only for a moment, and then fell back. We waited for a moment. He showed no further sign of life, so we drove through. We made several photographs, and when we went back through the gate, the man was still asleep, and he didn't raise his head as we passed. He didn't need any business that day, we concluded, at least not badly enough to assume a vertical position.

The people along the river fish, farm, and hunt a little. Many are self-employed; they cut pulpwood. Most of the open lands thereabout are owned by paper companies. But the swamp, of course, is a government-protected preserve. The Suwannee has never been of commercial importance, at least not in Georgia. Steamboats once traveled upstream from the Suwannee's mouth to Ellaville, Florida, a distance of 130 miles. But the steamboats have long since disappeared.

The principal man-made point of interest on the river is

the Stephen Collins Foster Memorial Museum at White
Springs, Florida, some 25 miles below the Georgia border.
It contains a wealth of Foster memorabilia—books, manu-
scripts, music scores, letters, paintings, and pianos. It draws
upward of 500,000 visitors a year. Being familiar with Foster's
song, and seeing the river, people are skeptical when informed
that Foster himself never actually saw the Suwannee. But
the song was no more than a happy, accidental marriage of
nature and imagination, a marriage that in all probability will
be as everlasting as the quiet river itself.

.. 6 ..

COOSA

By Katherine Barnwell

For centuries a lively trading center has flourished in northwest Georgia at the site where the Coosa River is formed by the merging waters of two other rivers—the murky red-brown Etowah and the swift greenish Oostanaula. Lithe bronze-skinned Cherokee Indians, who paddled slender canoes on the three rivers, used to stop and trade at the Indian town of Chiaha, where the city of Rome is now located. There the Cherokees had a post office, appropriately known as "Head of the Coosa," two ferries, and several large trading posts.

In 1540 the Spanish explorer Hernando de Soto, journeying from what is now South Carolina to the Mississippi River is believed to have followed the Oostanaula River to its junction with the Etowah. He and his followers—who arrived in this country 80 years before the landing of the Pilgrims—remained in the section about a month. Indians brought baskets of corn, gourds filled with bear oil, pots of honey, and a large quantity of game to replenish De Soto's supplies.

KATHERINE BARNWELL was born in Rome, Georgia, and grew up on a Coosa River farm. She was graduated from Shorter College in her home town and received a Bachelor of Journalism degree from the University of Missouri. After graduation she joined the *Atlanta Constitution* as a reporter and subsequently served as science editor. In 1957 she joined the staff of the *Atlanta Journal and Constitution Magazine*.

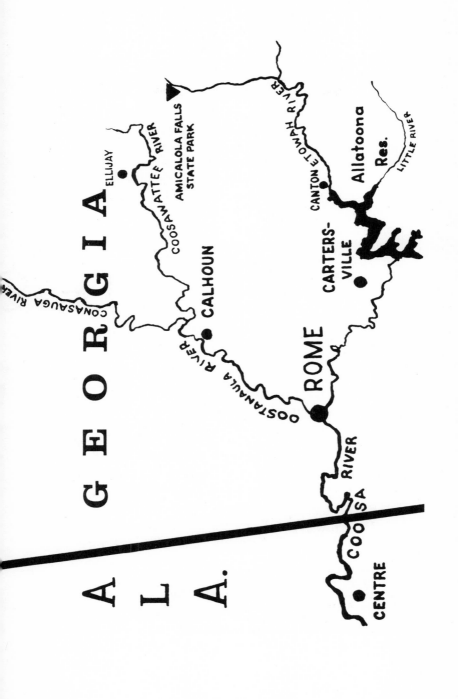

At the close of the 18th century white pioneers began to press the Indians out of northwest Georgia. In 1834 five white settlers visited the site where the Coosa is formed. They promptly decided it would be an ideal station for steamboat traffic—and they founded the town of Rome, named for the ancient Italian city. Rome, Georgia, soon became a thriving inland port. Colorful steamboats, carrying both passengers and cargo, plied the Coosa until early in the 20th century, when they were gradually abandoned as a mode of transportation.

Now at a ripe old age of 128 years, Rome is striving to become an inland port again. Rome civic leaders predict that the 587 miles from their city to Mobile Bay by way of the Coosa and Alabama rivers will be made navigable in 10 or 15 years. They believe huge barges, laden with such cargo as petroleum, chemicals, timber, ore, grain, and manufactured products, will be floating up and down the rivers before another two decades roll around.

T. Harley Harper of Rome, chairman of the Coosa Valley Area Planning and Development Commission, and Carl Collins, manager of the Rome-Floyd County Chamber of Commerce, maintain that modern commercial navigation will bring great new prosperity to the entire region. "The Coosa-Alabama river system is the largest undeveloped waterway in the Southeast," Mr. Harper points out. The Coosa has a greater water flow per day at Rome—an average of more than four billion gallons—than the Flint at Albany, the Ocmulgee at Macon, or the Chattahoochee at Atlanta.

The Etowah and the Oostanaula are Cherokee Indian words meaning "dead wood place" and "shoals or rock barrier," respectively—but there is no translation for Coosa in the Cherokee vocabulary. Mr. Harper and Mr. Collins, whose enthusiasm for the Coosa is in the best chamber-of-commerce tradition, suggest that the name means "the greatest." "We think it's the greatest," Mr. Harper observed with a grin, "and if anyone denies it, then he's not a true Cherokee Indian!"

Burgett Mooney, publisher of the *Rome News-Tribune*, is a member of the executive committee of the Coosa-Alabama River Improvement Association, which is working for development of a navigable channel from Rome to Mobile. "A great waterway for commercial navigation," he says, "definitely would promote industrial development, population growth, and improvement of the total economy of this region."

Actually, the Coosa—286 miles in length—doesn't remain long in Georgia. After winding for about 30 miles west of Rome it crosses into Alabama, flows southwest, and finally joins the Tallapoosa River between Wetumpka and Montgomery to form the Alabama River. North of Mobile the Alabama joins the Tombigbee to form the Mobile River, which flows into Mobile Bay.

Development of the Coosa and Alabama rivers already is well under way, but at least six new dams must be built on the two streams before Rome can be an inland port. Construction of the $32,000,000 Allatoona Dam and Reservoir on the Etowah River near Cartersville was an important step in the comprehensive development program. Besides providing electric power, the Allatoona project holds back flood waters of the upper Etowah and regulates the Coosa's flow downstream. The lake created by the dam affords vast recreational facilities. More than 2,000,000 people a year visit Allatoona and enjoy such activities as boating, water skiing, fishing, swimming, and camping.

The Allatoona Dam has greatly reduced flood damages at Rome. Since the dam was built, flood control benefits have averaged nearly $400,000 a year, according to an estimate by the U.S. Army Corps of Engineers. Construction of levees along the banks of the Etowah and the Oostanaula in downtown Rome in the 1930s also has helped prevent flooding and greatly enhanced property values in certain sections of the city.

The biggest flood on record in Rome was in April 1886, when the Coosa's flood stage reached 40.3 feet. That year a steamboat sailed up Broad Street—the city's main business thoroughfare then and now. The street was 10 feet under water. A picturesque covered bridge built of wood, which spanned the Etowah River on South Broad Street, was washed away by the same flood.

The Etowah River, which is 99 miles long, has its source in Lumpkin County, northwest of Dahlonega. It flows westward through five other counties—Dawson, Forsyth, Cherokee, Bartow, and Floyd—until it joins the Oostanaula at Rome. There is always a distinct difference in color between the two rivers at the juncture; the Oostanaula is much clearer than the mud-stained Etowah. The Coosa usually has a coffee-with-light-cream hue. Rome civic leaders blame the muddy color of the Etowah on mining companies in Cartersville. They say that silt from iron ore and other minerals mined in the area is dumped in the river, and makes the water many shades darker than it normally would be. Romans hope to persuade the companies to use other means of disposing of waste materials. They also are trying to get cities up and down the Oostanaula and Etowah to stop dumping their sewage in the rivers.

One of the tributaries of the Etowah is the Amicalola River —a clear, sparkling, mountain stream unspoiled by man. The river, a utopia for trout fishermen, gurgles merrily over a rocky bed. It is fed by Amicalola Falls, one of the state's beauty spots, in Dawson County.

Amicalola Falls, highest falls in Georgia, is formed by a creek which plunges 729 feet down the eastern side of Amicalola Ridge in a series of sparkling cascades. Many Georgians have never seen the falls because of its relative isolation, but there are roads leading to the top and the bottom.

The Oostanaula River is only 45 miles long. It is formed west of Calhoun in Gordon County by the confluence of the Coosawattee and Conasauga rivers, two pretty mountain streams.

Construction of a $38,000,000 dam on the Coosawattee River about 15 miles below Ellijay is expected to begin in 1962. The project—known as Carter's Dam—is another unit necessary in the development of the Coosa and Alabama river system. The dam, which will back up 2,550 acres of water in Murray and Gilmer counties, will help provide flood control and a constant navigation water supply at Rome. The new lake will be only about 40 miles northeast of Rome; mountains in the area will provide an impressive backdrop for the reservoir.

Rome is even closer—only 20 miles—to another lake, formed by the new Weiss Dam on the Coosa River near Centre, Alabama. Part of the 45-square-mile lake is backed up into Floyd County. Constructed by the Alabama Power Company, the Weiss Dam and lake are an integral part of the Alabama-Coosa development.

The Alabama Power Company and the federal government are co-operating in the development of the Rome-to-Mobile waterway. The plan of development will make use of three hydro-electric dams which the power company built on the Coosa between 1910 and 1929. Weiss Dam was recently completed and three additional dams on the Coosa are to be constructed by 1968.

The U.S. Army Corps of Engineers will develop the Alabama River by constructing three new dams with locks—one navigation dam at Claiborne and two power-navigation dams at Jones Bluff and Millers Ferry. Planning funds for the Millers Ferry project in southwest Alabama have been appropriated, and construction plans are well under way. Upon completion of the dams on the Alabama River, the Corps of Engineers is expected to install locks in the power company's dams on the Coosa, and so provide a nine-foot navigable channel from Rome to the Port of Mobile. Congress still must appropriate many millions of dollars for the development.

The Corps of Engineers has estimated that a total of 4,681,000 tons of cargo could be moved on the waterway with an annual savings of $8,669,000. Of the total, 2,016,000 tons could be moved on the Alabama River between Mobile and Montgomery—and 2,665,000 tons could be transported on the Coosa between Montgomery and Rome. The savings would result from the low-cost water transportation rates on such materials as petroleum products, minerals, chemicals, fertilizer, grain, transformers, and other manufactured products.

Officials of the Coosa-Alabama River Improvement Association predict that complete development of the waterway would result in the employment of 55,000 new industrial workers in the river basin in the next few years. They also predict there would be 186,000 new inhabitants, with 30,350 new school children, and an increase of 90,750 in passenger car registrations and of $251,350,000 in retail sales per year.

During the middle and latter part of the 19th century steamboats and barges on the Coosa carried such cargo as baled cotton, pig iron, country produce, dried animal skins, and live fowls in large baskets. Water transportation greatly boosted the economy of the region then, as it is expected to do again. Some of the river boats which plied the Coosa were the *Alabama*, the *Cherokee*, the *Clara Belle*, the *Conasauga*, the *Dixie*, the *Magnolia*, and the *Sidney Smith*. There were often races between steamboats on the Coosa. The *Sidney Smith* defeated the *Magnolia* in an exciting race witnessed by hundreds of people.

The first steamboat built in Rome was the *Pennington*; Captain F. M. Coulter made it for Colonel C. M. Pennington. Lengths of pine wood, cut and piled at landings along the river, were used as fuel to power many of the old steamboats; coal also was used as fuel. Streams of smoke and bright sparks poured from the tall smokestacks on the boats. The steamboat's engine turned the single paddle wheel at the stern.

In his *History of Rome and Floyd County*, George M. Battey wrote that one steamboat brought many federal prisoners up the Coosa from Greensport, Alabama, during the Civil War. He also recorded that a company of Confederate soldiers was transported by steamboat from Bell's Ferry to Rome en route to Virginia.

Many people were passengers on cargo-carrying steamboats. The lower deck was for Negro slaves, river trappers, and riverside farmers; the upper deck was for "nice" passengers, according to one account of steamboat travel.

Each stateroom on a steamboat had a pair of berths—the lower one was wider for "fat" guests. In the staterooms were big oil lamps, washstands, and large tin pitchers of water. The rooms had doors to a hall or "eatery" in the middle of the boat. Fine food was served there to guests. On the menu were such delicacies as cold ham, cold roast beef, fresh fish, hot biscuits, cornpone, country sweet butter, game in season, country preserves, and pickles.

The last steamboat on the Coosa was owned by Hugh E. Green, a native Roman known to all his friends as "Piggy." Mr. Green bought the boat from the federal government; its original cost was about $40,000. He remodeled the boat in the 1930s, changed its name from *Leota* to *Annie M.*, and used it to take passengers on sightseeing trips.

"The river was still navigable from Rome to Gadsden then," Mr. Green recalls. "It's 129 miles by river between the two towns. I used to go down the river in 13 hours in that old steamboat, but it took two to four days to come back upstream. It took longer when the river was high. I could take about 200 passengers on the *Annie M.*, which had two decks. It was 147 feet long, 33 feet wide and had a 122-ton displacement. After about three years I sold the boat—and it later sank at Gadsden. That was the last of the steamboats on the Coosa."

The few boats on the Coosa today are mainly small ones used for fishing. Fishermen pull catfish, bream, bass, and crappie from the river.

There is one houseboat on the Coosa, built by a Rome fireman, Henry Johnson, during his off-duty hours. The fireman—known as "Son" Johnson—spent two years and about $4,000 constructing the houseboat, which is 46 feet long and 16 feet wide. No one knows exactly when the houseboat will be joined by modern cargo-loaded barges on the Coosa-Alabama waterway. It is not absolutely certain that the projected development will be completed. But Rome's civic leaders are optimistic; they believe Congress will realize the value of the development program.

Twelve northwest Georgia counties have organized the Coosa Valley Area Planning and Development Commission, with headquarters in Rome. Purpose of the organization is the development of the section in six fields of activity—agriculture, industry, local and regional planning, governmental affairs, tourist promotion, and water resource development. A navigable Rome-to-Mobile water route is one of the objectives of the commission. As Chairman Harley Harper summed up: "Our rivers are God-given assets, but we are not using them to best advantage. Commercial navigation on the Coosa would mean a new era of prosperity and growth for Georgia and Alabama."

.. 7 ..

~~~~~~

FLINT

~~~~~~

BY KATHERINE BARNWELL

GEORGIA'S Flint River, which flows through or alongside 19 counties, covers 330 miles as it winds its way down the state. You can't put a price tag on a river—but the Flint undoubtedly is one of the state's biggest assets. It begins as a small unimpressive stream in College Park. Well fed by other creeks and rivers, it grows as it travels south to meet the Chattahoochee River and form Lake Seminole at the Jim Woodruff Dam on the Georgia-Florida border. It flows through the town of Bainbridge, a thriving inland port.

The Flint has many faces. It is a swift, tawny-colored river where fishermen find bream, bass, catfish—and relaxation. It is a meandering, tree-lined stream, which draws water skiers, boat enthusiasts, and summer picnickers in great numbers when the weather is suitable for outdoor recreation. It is a commercial waterway where powerful little towboats push tremendous barges heavily loaded with cargo—such as corn, flour, and sulphur.

It nourishes great lakes; the river's force is harnessed to produce electric power which turns the wheels of industry and makes possible the marvels of modern living. It rushes under highway bridges. At one point near Marshallville, it is a formidable barrier which can be crossed by motorists only on an old-fashioned ferry. It twists and gurgles through the beautiful Flint River Valley where the soil is rich and farmers produce some of the world's best peaches, pecans, peanuts, and livestock.

At times, it is a terrifying torrent of flooding water that rapidly overspreads low-lying farmlands and laps at houses along its banks. An 88-year-old woman who lives in view of the Flint near Ideal, Georgia, shook her head and said, "When hit floods, hit's an awful sight to see!"

Roger Streetman of Ideal recalls that in 1927 the Flint flooded the nearby town of Montezuma—and some men paddled a boat into the movie theater there. "Montezuma and some other towns along the Flint have dikes and levees now so the water doesn't flood 'em as bad as it used to," he points out.

The U.S. Army Corps of Engineers built a levee along Beaver Creek at Montezuma to protect low-lying sections of that town from floods caused by back waters of the Flint. A levee, flood wall, and pumping station were completed in 1958 at a cost of $150,000. The project already has greatly reduced Montezuma's flood losses and enhanced property values.

For at least two centuries—probably longer—the Flint River has played an important role in Georgia. In 1765 there was an Indian trading post on the Flint exactly where Bainbridge is now located; the site was in Spanish territory at that time. Frank Jones of Bainbridge, 85-year-old retired chairman of the First State National Bank, said the trading post was operated by an Englishman named James Burgess who had an Indian wife.

During the War of 1812 both the British and the Americans had forts near the junction of the Flint and Chattahoochee rivers, Mr. Jones points out. One of the landings on the river is still known as the "British Burying Grounds."

THE first steamboat that plied the Flint River was the *Fannie*, which went to Bainbridge in 1827. The next year the *Fannie* went up the Chattahoochee to Columbus. The boat eventually blew up. Many steamers went up and down the Flint and the Chattahoochee during the 1800s; they carried both passengers and cargo. Grady Marchant and D. R. Bower compiled a list of boats that operated between 1828 and 1889 on the rivers. They had such picturesque names as the *Bessie Clary*, the *Flint Bride*, the *Hard Times*, the *Free Trader*, and the *Joke*.

Steamers frequently went as far up the Flint River as Albany, more than 50 miles northeast of Bainbridge. A history of Dougherty County records that life in Albany during the 19th century "was centered around the river." The Flint was described as the town's main "highway." When word was circulated that a steamboat was expected, the whole community took on new life. And when a boat's whistle sounded, nearly every man, woman, and child in town went down to the river at the end of Broad Street to greet it.

The late Mrs. Adelaide Jackson, a pioneer resident of Albany, once told a newspaperman that she was on a boat which sank in the Flint in 1844. She and one of her children —a baby at the time—were passengers on the *Viola* when it struck a hidden rock in the river and sank. She said everyone on the boat remained calm, and all aboard were taken off safely before it went down. There also were 1,000 bags of cotton aboard, but they floated and were recovered. Mrs. Jackson described the *Viola* as a fine boat, the largest of the steamers that plied the Flint in her day. Boats and barges carrying commercial cargo today require a deeper channel of water than did the steamboats of the 19th century. However, many steamers, like the *Viola,* did run aground or sink when the river was low.

Modern commercial navigation on the Flint was made possible in 1957 by the completion of the $46,000,000 Jim Woodruff Lock and Dam at the southwest corner of Georgia— where the Flint and the Chattahoochee merge and flow into Florida's Apalachicola River. The project by the U.S. Corps of Engineers also provided for a channel at least nine feet deep and 100 feet wide as far as Bainbridge—28 miles up the river.

In 1960 more than 50,000 tons of cargo were brought into Bainbridge by barges pushed up the river by sturdy little towboats. Deasy Rahn, manager of the Bainbridge State Docks, is optimistic about future increases in cargo tonnage. Products now arriving in Bainbridge by water include asphalt, flour, corn, sulphur, propane gas, sugar, oyster shells for use in chicken feed, and chemicals for insecticides. Outgoing shipments on the Flint to date have been insignificant, but Mr. Rahn expects them to increase. He points out that pine timber from south Georgia soon will be sent by barge from Bainbridge to New Orleans. "The number of commodities that could be economically handled through the port of Bainbridge is tremendous," Mr. Rahn stresses.

Further development of the Flint River will be necessary to make Albany an inland port and to control flood waters up and down the river valley. The Flint River Development Association, headed by John Phillips of Albany, is working hard to get the government to build additional dams on the Flint. Mr. Phillips points out that every town and community in the Flint River Valley would benefit from this development.

Walter R. Brown, manager of the Albany Chamber of Commerce, cites a preliminary survey by the U.S. Corps of Engineers which showed that development of the river for navigation to Albany would be feasible. A comprehensive survey of the proposed Flint project is now under way.

"We expect to get a favorable report from the comprehensive survey soon," Mr. Brown says. "We hope to get 'planning' money in 1962 and 'starting' money in 1963. To make the Flint navigable to Albany they say will take two dams between here and Bainbridge and one or two up the river in the vicinity of Thomaston. Estimates are that it would cost 75 to 100 million dollars to complete the project —but it would mean over 7 million dollars a year in savings to shippers. The economic benefits would make it worthwhile."

Albany leaders point out that additional dams on the Flint not only would open a whole new avenue of commerce and trade by inland waterway, but they also would provide these benefits: electric power, water, recreation areas, and

flood control. They say dams up the river would control
flood waters so that "our homes and businesses would no
longer be threatened by the power of the river to destroy
life and property."

"The economic benefits of transportation on the Flint
already have been demonstrated at Bainbridge," Mr. Rahn
says. "Water rates are about 20 to 30 per cent lower than
normal freight rates," he explains. "Some very large barges
can carry as much cargo as 140 rail cars. That's where water
transportation has it over rail. You can carry so many more
tons per mile on the water."

State docks at Bainbridge were built at a total cost of
about $1,000,000. Mr. Rahn says 400 feet of docks are al-
ready developed but an additional 1,300 feet will be built
in the next 10 years. Several industries at Bainbridge also have
their own dock facilities. In a typical month 33 barges brought
various products into the port. "We have nine full-time employees and 24 part-time employees at the state docks," Mr.
Rahn reports. "We charge for services—loading, unloading
and warehouse storage—and we haven't lost money. We're
operating in the black. We have now enough warehouse
space to hold three barge loads; about 320,000 square feet
of additional warehouse space will be built as needed."

Flour is shipped regularly to Bainbridge all the way from
Minnesota by barge; it comes down the Mississippi to New
Orleans, moves through the intracoastal waterway to Apalachicola, Florida, and up the Apalachicola and Flint rivers
to Bainbridge. The flour in 100-pound bags is lifted from
the barge by a crane, placed on pallets, and moved by fork
lifts to the warehouse. Then the flour is transported by truck
to bakeries in south Georgia.

The two captains of one towboat, the *Scintilla*, which
pushed a barge loaded with flour to Bainbridge, say they
average about seven miles an hour on the Flint River. Bill
Plemmons of Columbus, Georgia, and O. F. Barnes of Pana-

Etowah River near Canton.

The steamboat *Annie M.* on the Oostanaula River at Rome in the 1930s. The Fifth Avenue bridge and the courthouse tower are in the background.

Woodruff Dam on the Flint at the Georgia-Florida line, where the Flint and the Chattahoochee make Lake Seminole.

The Chattahoochee at the Atlanta water-works plant and the city's intake station at Bolton.

The Chattahoochee at Robertstown before rushing down through the hills of Habersham County.

Oglethorpe visited the Indians at Coweta Town, near these swift shoals on the Chattahoochee between West Point and Columbus.

Sailboats on Lake Lanier.

Holiday Marina on Lake Lanier.

The packet *Queen City*, with 700 bales of cotton, tied up at Fort Gaines landing in 1900. The Walter F. George Dam is just above this point.

Looking from Phenix City, Alabama, into Columbus.

ma City, Florida, report they make a round trip from New Orleans to Bainbridge in about eight days. "One of us steers while the other sleeps," Captain Barnes explains. "We have two other men on the boat. One is our cook, engineer, and deck hand, and the other is a deck hand.

"We make about 27 turns on the Flint River between the Woodruff Dam and Bainbridge. There are one or two turns every mile. Because the water is backed up by the dam, the Flint River runs like a lake. Coming up the Apalachicola River below the dam the current is so strong we make only about four miles an hour—but we do better than nine an hour going down."

Each towboat has a ship-to-shore radio phone so that it can keep in touch with personnel at the lock and dam and at the Bainbridge docks. A captain can report exactly where his towboat is at any time because the channel is clearly marked by buoys.

Although running a towboat—pushing heavily loaded barges —isn't as exciting as taking a luxury cruise, Captain Barnes and Captain Plemmons say they enjoy their work. "We have good food on the boat—anything we want," Captain Barnes points out. "I've worked on boats of all kinds for the past 37 years; I've had 'em sink, blow up, and everything. Running a towboat on a river is pretty simple—just like running up and down a highway. But it's a little slower. I like being on the go all the time."

"If I *didn't* like it," Captain Plemmons says succinctly, "I'd quit." His chief complaint about his trips on the Flint is that fishermen and water skiers sometimes get in the way.

The boat captains praised the "fast" operation of the lock at the Woodruff Dam. They say they can go through it in 20 minutes, whereas it often takes an hour and a half to go through other locks. At the Woodruff Dam there's a concrete powerhouse containing three 10,000-kilowatt generators. The power plant produces an average annual energy output of about 220,000,000 kilowatt hours—enough to serve 69,000 homes. In one year the power was sold by the Southeastern Power Administration for about $1,360,000.

The Corps of Engineers has provided facilities for visitors at the dam site and has built access roads, parking areas, and boat launching ramps around the reservoir—Lake Seminole. The lake covers 37,500 acres and has a 243-mile shoreline. Various state, county, and municipal agencies are developing other recreational facilities. Visitors to the lake number about 1,300,000 a year.

The only county-owned and -operated electric power plant in Georgia is at Lake Blackshear, formed by the Flint River near Cordele, Georgia. The Crisp County Power Commission operates the hydro-electric plant which serves the 17,000 people in the county. In 1958 a new steam plant was put in operation alongside the hydro-electric plant. Lake Blackshear, which is six miles from Cordele, covers 8,000 acres and has many recreational facilities. They include picnic areas, a recreational building with restaurant facilities, and overnight cabins.

Another dam on the Flint River forms the Georgia Power Lake near Albany. The water is harnessed to produce power, and nearby is the Plant Mitchell steam generator. The lake also is used for recreation.

Various industries are scattered up and down the Flint; they now use the water for such purposes as cooling. If the river is made navigable to Albany, more industries undoubtedly will establish plants along the river to take advantage of the commercial waterway.

Travelers in Georgia cross many bridges over the Flint, but the river may well be one of the state's least publicized natural resources. Frequently the motorist doesn't know what river he's crossing because there are no signs designating it. There is a new four-lane bridge over the Flint on U.S. Highways 84 and 27 at Bainbridge (the Flint's name isn't marked there yet, either). Actually the bridge is "twins" because there are two identical bridges—one for traffic each way. The over-all length of the twin bridges, including the approaches, is more than 900 feet. The new bridge is in striking contrast to old Underwood's Ferry which crosses the Flint south of Marshallville. The battered wooden ferry, powered by a 1938 automobile motor, is on Georgia Highway 127. The State Highway Department reports it is one of the last two ferries in operation in Georgia; the only other one is Dame's Ferry over the Ocmulgee River on Georgia Highway 18.

Lester Cromer took over the job of running Underwood's Ferry early in 1961 when his brother became seriously ill; his brother had operated the ferry for seven years. "I don't know how old this ferry is," said Mr. Cromer, "but it's old. Lots of people cross this ferry just to see how it rides." The ferry is guided by two large cables attached to trees on each side of the river. When the ferry's car motor is started, the cables turn around a drum—made from mowing machine blades—and the ferry moves to the opposite bank. A crossing takes only a minute and 10 seconds.

"Saturday and Sunday are the busiest days," Mr. Cromer says. "Some Sundays I go back and forth all day. I'm on call seven days a week, 24 hours a day. I live in that house where I can see the cars come from both directions; if a driver wants to cross at night, he just blows his horn and I get up and go take him across.

"Once a car almost rolled off because the driver forgot to put on his brakes. He had gotten out, but his wife was still in the car when it started rolling. I caught hold of the car and yelled—and the man jumped in and yanked on his brakes just in time."

Mr. Cromer, who has five children of his own, says children get a big kick out of crossing.

The Flint River flooded in February of 1961. It rose 24

feet above normal, and the ferry was out of operation for a week. Mr. Cromer said logs as big as the front end of a car came down the river, causing one of the cables to break. The ferry was almost carried away by the swift current, but Mr. Cromer was able to anchor it.

Mr. Cromer probably spends more time on the Flint River than any other man. When he's not running the ferry, he's fishing from the banks. His family has "two or three messes" of fish a week, and he sells what they don't want to eat. Sizing up the Flint and speaking the sentiments of many Georgians, he concluded: "It's a pretty good river."

. . 8 . .

~~~~~~

CHATTAHOOCHEE

~~~~~~

BY RALPH MCGILL

Up above Poplar Stump Gap, where the great rock rim of the Blue Ridges marks the southwestern border of the huge Highland area, a small trickle of water spills from the rocks. It splashes down to form a small pool. Two small streams, not more than two or three inches wide, flow from it, splashing down into the laurel thickets.

Thus begins the Chattahoochee River. Once in the thickets it is joined by other streams, and soon there is what might be called a small mountain creek. Others hurry to merge with it. In Habersham, Rabun, White, Towns, Union, and Lumpkin counties, there are waters which flow into it.

In the mountains it is a river for poets. Sidney Lanier, ill and slowly wasting away with tuberculosis, sat by its banks near Helen. He saw it in his mind's eye all the way to the sea, and gave it literary immortality:

RALPH MCGILL was born at Soddy, Tennessee. He began his newspaper career when he was working his way through Vanderbilt University by writing police news and politics for the *Nashville Banner*. He served in the Marines in World War I, became sports editor of the *Banner* in 1923, and was named sports editor of the *Atlanta Constitution* in 1929. He was chosen editor in 1942 and succeeded to publisher in 1960. His column has appeared daily in the *Atlanta Constitution* for 32 years and is syndicated in many newspapers in America. Among awards he has received was the Pulitzer Prize for Outstanding Editorial Writing in 1958.

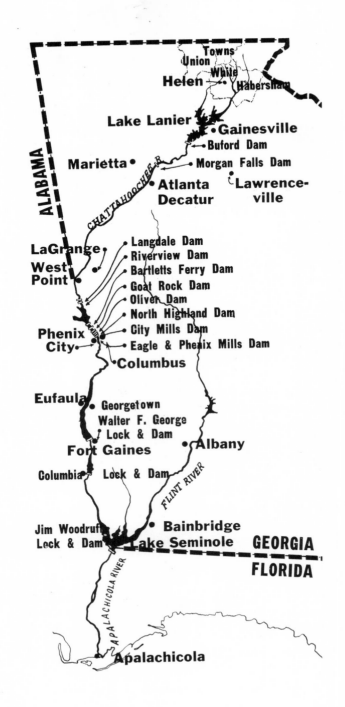

> *Out of the hills of Habersham,*
> *Down the valleys of Hall,*
> *I hurry amain to reach the plain,*
> *Run the rapid and leap the fall,*
> *Split at the rock and together again,*
> *Accept my bed, or narrow or wide,*
> *And flee from folly on every side*
> *With a lover's pain to attain the plain*
> *Far from the hills of Habersham,*
> *Far from the valleys of Hall.*

The river did turn many wheels. It gave the state its first complex of industry at Columbus. It still is a river for the poets. The Cherokees put the name on it which the English spelled phonetically Chat-Chochee, Chat-a-Hotchee, or in some approximation of the Indian words. The phrase meant, in a free translation, "river of the painted rock," a name with poetry in it. There were rocks in the upper reaches stained red and pink by nature. If the Cherokees believed this to be the work of the gods they may not have been wrong.

From its beginnings in the Appalachian Blue Ridges until it reaches Columbus, the Chattahoochee is one of the oldest rivers in the Southeast. From the old Coweta Falls (near Columbus) close by which was the old war-town of the Creeks, the river is younger, geologists say, by many hundreds of thousands of years.

In the dim geologic ages rivers "pirated" one another with frequency. They would do so today, if man did not impose dams and controls.

Once upon a time, say geologists, the Chattahoochee was a mighty river indeed. It included what is now the Chattooga and the Tallapoosa. The drainage changes took place a million years or so ago, but geologists are reasonably sure of what happened. The Atlantic coast line was then at the approximate position of Montgomery, Columbus, Macon, and Augusta. The huge river at that time would have entered the sea at a point not far northeast of Montgomery. With the new sea at this level, the tributaries flowing from the north began to cut their beds in a manner best illustrated by the formation of a gully in a field. It is cut backward, so to speak, and deepest, where the water is strongest, just as gullies are deeper where the heaviest surge of collected rain water flows. As the new ocean receded toward the present Atlantic and Gulf coasts, the rivers cut easily into the softer soils of the coastal plains, making wide valley courses. Shorter streams, not so sluggish as the larger and longer Chattahoochee, of course, cut deeper and more swiftly.

One such stream, geologists say, cut into the valley of the Chattahoochee above West Point, diverting the Chatta-hoochee into the Gulf by way of what is called the Apa-lachicola. The Flint, Ocmulgee, Oconee, and Savannah, a million years or so before they had names, were likewise busy with their own evolutionary struggles. The Savannah, called the Tugaloo in its upper reaches, intercepted the Chattahoochee somewhere around the Habersham-Stephens county line, tak-ing these headwaters into what became the Tugaloo-Savannah system.

Geologists like to think what a vast roaring there must have been, and what a spectacular sight it was, when in those early days of our part of the new world, a small tributary of what is called the Tugaloo intersected the Tallulah and set it to cutting the Tallulah gorge in its rush into the Tugaloo system. Once upon a time the Tallulah flowed down past the present gorge and falls and turned southwest, going then down to the valley of Deep Creek and the Soque River where it became the leading tributary to the Chattahoochee.

To this day, between Atlanta and Gainesville, some of the headwaters of seaward-flowing streams are close to the Chat-tahoochee, but dams and modern engineering prevent any "piracy" of interception. So it is, as geologists construct the ancient evidence, that the oldest part of the Chattahoochee remains in Georgia, its channel following the narrow Gulf-

Atlantic divide. It flows first through the pleasant and beautiful valley of Nacoochee, where most historians agree De Soto halted after he had at last found what we call Rabun Gap and emerged from his long, arduous passage through the seemingly endless folds of the Appalachians into the Piedmont region. From there the river sets out on its peculiar, unorthodox course, southwest across the state.

From Nacoochee the river flows to Clarkesville and there steps down in swift cascades to the Atlanta plateau. Nowhere is this plateau more than 50 miles wide. In places it is as narrow as 35. Yet, it stretches for about 100 miles, composed of two fairly distinct levels, or benches, with about 250 feet difference in elevation. The plateau's terrain is pleasant. It bears the principal railways and highways. It is dotted with attractive cities—Gainesville, Atlanta, Carrollton, Newnan, and West Point being the better known.

The most striking feature of this plateau is the great trench which the river cut in the dim and distant past. This trench ranges from 150 to 400 or more feet in depth and from two to five miles in width from rim to rim. For a short distance below Roswell the trench is almost a gorge. There is some evidence that the trench, or valley, is a double one with a deeper, more narrow river course cut into the floor of a wider one which dates back to the ages when the Chattahoochee was a mighty river.

Below Franklin, in Heard County, where once the slave-poled barges came for cotton, the Chattahoochee begins its cross swing and steps down to the Greenville Plateau, so called after the seat of Meriwether County. This plateau extends well into Alabama. The river flows across it as far south as Columbus.

It there nears the Flint, which rises in College Park. The Flint cuts through the Pine Mountain ridges near Woodbury, Georgia. It had a great struggle in the ancient days when it was becoming a river. Within the space of six miles the Flint had to slash three gorges through the complicated low loops of the rocky ridges. But though the two rivers are near each other, the Flint has miles to go before it joins the Chattahoochee. At Columbus is the fall line. For years the steamboats came there in considerable numbers. The writer has talked with men who worked on them. They recalled the difficult channel, the several boats sunk by running on hidden snags. They remembered the fine meals, and how, in the autumn and winter, hunters would come to the landings and sell hundreds of quail at a cent apiece and offer choice cuts of deer meat at low prices.

The first steamer to make the long journey from the Gulf to Columbus was the *Fannie* in 1828. The *Steubenville* came the same year. In 1829 the *Virginia* appeared and set a record by making the trip from Apalachicola to Columbus in 38 hours. In December of 1829 she took 400 bales of cotton from Columbus to New Orleans. In 1834 there were six steamers on the river from Columbus to the sea.

The Civil War saw Federal gunboats on the lower stretches of the river. They operated frequently to Eufaula, Alabama. The Confederate gunboat *Chattahoochee* was built at Columbus. She was blown up in April 1865, by the Federals. Steamboating slowly died out and by 1921 was ended. But in February of 1939, a tug towed a barge containing 150,000 gallons of gasoline to Columbus. In the years ahead, as dams are built, ocean barges will come to Atlanta.

Below Columbus the Chattahoochee flows into the flat of the coastal plain. It moves by Fort Benning, where thousands of troops trained for the second great world war and where General George Patton formed his tank battalions. The first test of rubber tank pontoons was on the Chattahoochee. Flowing on, the Chattahoochee goes past historic Eufaula in old Barbour County, past Fort Gaines and Columbia, the latter now well back from the river, and so on until its union with the Flint at the southwest corner of Georgia.

In Florida the river flows past the town of Chattahoochee, where the swamps begin along the river, by Blountstown, and, finally, by the mouth of Brothers River. There the river slows for the bay, where the town of Apalachicola still holds to the old dream of becoming a great seaport.

Early Spanish explorers fixed the name Apalachicola on the lower stretch of the river. French explorers also paddled canoes up it to the Indian towns at Coweta and Cusseta. But the Spanish made the most persistent effort to get their foot in the Creek Nation door and extend their bases up from St. Augustine. In 1679, Friar Juan Ocon attempted to set up a mission near Coweta. He was ordered out. In March of 1681 two Franciscans and seven soldiers rowed up the Chattahoochee to the Cowetas. It was the first armed expedition to use the river. The mission was ordered out in May.

In 1670 the British founded Charleston, and the great wrestling match for the New World was begun in earnest with France, Britain, and Spain as major contestants. By 1686 the Spanish and their missions were gone from the Georgia coast. But later, Indian wars brought the Spanish back to Coweta on the Chattahoochee. In London decision was reached to establish a buffer colony against the Spanish. Georgia was founded.

History has it that southeast America was saved for the British by General Oglethorpe's defeat of the Spanish at Bloody Marsh. But the battle could not have been won without a heroic journey to the Cowetas on the Chattahoochee by General Oglethorpe three years before the battle at Bloody Marsh. One is awed today in thinking of that long 300-mile trip through heat, swamps, unexplored wilderness, and rivers. At Coweta Town—in what is now Russell County, Alabama— General Oglethorpe met with the leaders of some 20,000 Indians. The general attended their ceremonies, drank "the Black Drink" and won them over. He then visited other towns on and near the Chattahoochee. A treaty was made. It endured all through the "War of Jenkins' Ear," or King George's War, that followed. Without these friendly Indians, Georgia, and perhaps Carolina, might have been lost. The destiny of the new colony was determined at Coweta Town on the Chattahoochee in August 1739.

There are many stories of the Chattahoochee's past. There are others to come when the dams are built and the ocean barges come to docks at cities along the way. She is not a large river, or a great one, if we think of the Mississippi, the Ohio, or the Tennessee, but she nonetheless is a river for poets, for recreation, for providing Atlanta and other cities with water, and for the economic, utilitarian plans of the future. There is plenty of length to her, if there are not great width and depth. She stretches 436 miles in a series of sinuous curves, tumbling rapids, placid meanderings. No other river in the state is as long.

The Walter F. George and Columbia dams are expected to bring navigation to Columbus in 1963 providing docks for ocean barges and the tough, fast tugs loaded with heavy goods and, in time, oil.

Navigation to Atlanta is practical but at considerable cost. Burton Bell, information specialist for the U.S. Army Corps of Engineers, and Caughey Culpepper, general manager of the Atlanta Freight Bureau, predict Atlanta one day will be an inland port. The fact that it is already one of the nation's major distribution cities will, in time, make it so. The problem is a simple, if costly, one, best illustrated by arithmetic. At Columbus the river is 190 feet above sea level. West Point, only 25 miles upriver but up a steep slope, is 372 feet higher. From there the rise is only 174 feet to Atlanta, where the waterworks intake pipe is 736 feet above sea level. Expensive dams and locks will be needed to care for the difference in elevation. But, already there is a compelling necessity to construct one or more dams between West Point and Atlanta to care for the flood provision problem. When these are built—and studies are being made—they will include facilities for installing locks for future navigation. The next ones will make Atlanta a port.

Opposition to Chattahoochee River navigation from the Gulf to Atlanta stems from the shortsighted who think in narrow terms of the cost for such transport. River barges are really one of the by-products of the chief need for the dams. The Buford Dam affords ample illustration. Completion of that dam gave to the state its finest playground in Lake Lanier. In 1960 it attracted 5,119,000 visitors—all of whom spent money. There is nothing intangible about the economic benefits in cold cash from recreation areas. In addition, Lake Lanier has revolutionized the area about it. It has brought hundreds of new businesses into being. It has stimulated a building boom. The sale, maintenance, and service of boats is a multimillion-dollar business. This alone will pay for the dam. But, in addition, we must include the value of land protected from floods. Until it is so protected, that land cannot be put to use for farming, homes, or industry.

Nor is this all. All cities are growing. Hence there is a steadily increasing demand for water. Industries require huge amounts of water. The dams, which store and conserve water, will, in time, pay for themselves by retaining water. It is neither honest nor constructive to think of river transport as bearing the whole cost of the necessary dams. Even if there were to be no barges the dams would be a requirement of the future. If it were not for the Chattahoochee River and its dams the state of Georgia would be much poorer and its future less bright. Atlanta long ago would have been in serious difficulty because of water shortages.

Eight Georgia Power Company plants on the river in operation at the start of 1962 were producing more than five billion kilowatts per year, and two new plants under construction were to bring the total output to almost ten billion kilowatts. What this means to industry and to cities of the state is obvious.

The Atlanta Water Works takes an average of 74,000,000 gallons of water per day from the Chattahoochee. On peak days in summer it has run as high as 110,000,000 gallons daily. The water works, according to General Manager Paul Weir, can supply 2,000,000 persons, so well have the plans been made and executed. Intake of Atlanta's water is at Bolton, on the west side of Atlanta, near Ridgewood and DeFoor roads. This was the old gateway to the Cherokee Nation. During the Civil War a boatyard did business there.

In addition to Atlanta, water-works systems taking water from the Chattahoochee are those of Gainesville, Buford, West Point, and Columbus, and the counties of DeKalb, Gwinnett, and Cobb.

Some years ago former Mayor James Nichols of Apalachicola gave Atlanta a 1,000-pound anchor, inscribed "The Port of Apalachicola salutes the Port of Atlanta." On the day the ocean tugs and barges come the anchor will be a part of the celebration. And that day is a part of the river's future.